# WHOLE PERSON HEALTH

## MINDFUL LIVING ACROSS THE LIFESPAN

MARIA NAPOLI » STEVE PETERSON

Ph.D.

M.Ed., MAIS

**Kendall Hunt**
publishing company

Front cover photos and section opener photo: courtesy of Maria Napoli

Back cover photos (top to bottom): courtesy of Moto Photo, Kelly Speir, and Tina Fasano-Cucci, respectively

4-Step MAC Guide logo: courtesy of Maria Napoli

The following interior images are from Shutterstock.com: Spotlight © Michael D Brown; Exclamation point © Palto; Check mark © CoraMax; Floor shapes © Asfia; Yoga posture © Ridkous Mykhailo; Newspaper © iQoncept; Tips for Wellbeing © arka38.

**Kendall Hunt**
publishing company
www.kendallhunt.com
*Send all inquiries to:*
4050 Westmark Drive
Dubuque, IA 52004-1840

Copyright © 2016 by Maria Napoli and Steve Peterson

ISBN 978-1-5249-3417-0

Printed in the United States of America

# Dedication

This book is dedicated to our readers
who have learned to live mindfully and are willing to take risks
and dream beyond their imagination.

# Contents

**Acknowledgments** . . . . . . . . . . . . . . . . . . . . . . . . . . . . . . . . . . . . . . . . . . . . . . . . vii

**Prologue** . . . . . . . . . . . . . . . . . . . . . . . . . . . . . . . . . . . . . . . . . . . . . . . . . . . . ix

**Chapter 1**    Mindfulness Across the Lifespan . . . . . . . . . . . . . . . . . . . . . . . . . 1
*Jamie Valderrama*

**Chapter 2**    Developing a Mindful Ego: The Power of Emotional Intelligence. . . 23
*Steve Peterson*

**Chapter 3**    The Positive Effects of Exercise Across the Lifespan . . . . . . . . . . . . 55
*Steve Peterson*

**Chapter 4**    The Healing Power of Play, Laughter, and Humor . . . . . . . . . . . . . 79
*Steve Peterson*

**Chapter 5**    Healthy Relationships Across the Lifespan . . . . . . . . . . . . . . . . . . . 101
*Tamara Rounds*

**Chapter 6**    The Benefits of Connecting with Nature . . . . . . . . . . . . . . . . . . . . 127
*Steve Peterson*

**Chapter 7**    The Benefits of the Human-Animal Relationship. . . . . . . . . . . . . . . 151
*Steve Peterson*

**Chapter 8**    Harmony Across the Lifespan: The Benefits of Music
Throughout Our Lives . . . . . . . . . . . . . . . . . . . . . . . . . . . . . . . . . . . . 173
*Charles Tyler and Eric Shetzen*

**Chapter 9**    The Artist Within Across the Lifespan. . . . . . . . . . . . . . . . . . . . . . . 189
*Olga Idriss Davis*

**Chapter 10**    Happiness: Journey and Destination . . . . . . . . . . . . . . . . . . . . . . 203
*Teri Kennedy*

**Answers to Chapter Questions** . . . . . . . . . . . . . . . . . . . . . . . . . . . . . . . . . . . . . 235

**Epilogue** . . . . . . . . . . . . . . . . . . . . . . . . . . . . . . . . . . . . . . . . . . . . . . . . . . . . 243

# Acknowledgments

*Photo courtesy of Maria Napoli*

As *Whole Person Health: Mindful Living Across the Lifespan* takes shape as a completed academic work embodying awareness, experience and personal/professional growth of a close-knit mindful movement, we would be remiss if we did not lend credence to those who made this experience possible. To our students who shared the positive impact that mindfulness had in their lives and helped guide the direction of our classroom instruction: we hold the deepest gratitude. Without them, we would be unable to assess the outcome of our work and see the fruits of our collective labor of love. To the knowledge facilitators, instructional staff and classroom leaders who brought this personal awareness to the pages of this book: your gifts took many shapes and the showcase of your talents had an impact that words cannot express. Thank you Jamie Valderrama, Tamara Rounds, Charles Tyler, Eric Shetzen, Olga Idriss Davis and Teri Kennedy. Not only did your contributions make this book possible, but also your unfaltering support, dedication and commitment to promoting our vision. A very special thank you to Susan Busatti Giangano for once again sharing her amazing musicianship and song-writing talents on the *Mindful MAC Meditations: Reflections Across the Lifespan*. Additional love and appreciation for the Kendall Hunt team for their continued support, guidance and ongoing confidence as we proudly release the third installment in the Stress Management Tools series. On a personal note, I must express a sincere heart-felt appreciation to my good friend and lifelong mentor, Maria. The personal transition from being her student to facilitating her vision in my own classroom has been an experience that has changed my life forever. Thank you for the opportunity and the blessings you have granted me. I am forever in your debt and have made a commitment to paying it forward. I also want to thank Kelly Speir for providing not only support during this writing process but also many hours of rough draft editing and input on the flow of the manuscript. In closing, the greatest appreciation goes to the readers and life-long learners who incorporate these teachings into their lives and share the beauty of a mindful existence with their families, loved ones and communities.

Maria Napoli and Steve Peterson

# Prologue

As you begin your journey through *Whole Person Health: Mindful Living Across the Lifespan* you will begin to reflect upon new ways to view your everyday life experiences. We know that basic needs must be met to survive, eat, drink, exercise, and earn enough money to meet those needs. Unfortunately, many of us lose sight of the amount of time we spend feeding our desires to earn more, hence, satisfying our thinking that more will make us happy. Throughout *Whole Person Health: Mindful Living Across the Lifespan* you will spend time nurturing your spirit of living; what excites you, nourishes your creativity, and sparks your passion.

If we go back to our earlier years before we understood what money was, you may remember playing with others, sitting with your pet for hours, coloring, and painting for the pure delight of experiencing the textures and colors, dancing aimlessly with laughter to music, and finding new ways to enjoy just about any ordinary activity. The sad news is many of us lose this perspective and forget the joy one can achieve by moving beyond the basic needs and exploring that part of us that can enjoy life more deeply and simply.

Think about the many people who love music and enjoy singing but hide out in the shower. The percentage of those who are born with perfect pitch does not represent even close to those who just love to sing for fun. This may be why karaoke has become so popular worldwide. Too often as adults we become observers rather than participants thinking that we need to be "good at" or successful at such activities as singing, dancing, painting, playing an instrument, photography, or hanging out with friends and family without an agenda.

From infancy to early childhood our worlds are balanced. We create, play, eat, laugh, and exercise all with spontaneity and in the moment, like a perfectly tuned instrument. Once we begin school, and for many children today school begins early, the drive toward achievement, structure, and skill development become more dominant. Play, laughter, and exercise too often take a back seat and are pigeon holed into time slots. The first thing to get cut in elementary schools is frequently physical education. I remember having physical education every day. Recess was a highlight of the day—playing with friends, running around, and letting go. In order for us to survive as healthy human beings we need to move. One might say that taking physical education away or minimizing a child's movement is against human nature.

It does not matter what group one belongs, I was raised in an urban-neighborhood working class family. I was fortunate to have a dad who was handy. There were times money was scarce and many of my play tools like skates and bicycles were hand-me-downs, softball was often played with a broom stick, forts were built from boxes when a neighbor received a washing machine or refrigerator. Those were treats to be cherished as our creativity flourished, imagination had no restrictions, and nature usually contributed to our décor with shrubs, rocks, and gravel. When I reflect back on those days I smile with joy as it was free spirited fun. It is truly the experiences we have, the ordinary and extraordinary, regardless of cost, that add to the spice of life. Mindfully stay present for all of your experiences using the Four Step MAC guide as you read through each chapter.

Mindfully

**A**cknowledge: All of your experiences without filters, just as they are.

**A**ttention: Notice your senses, body sensations, thoughts, and emotions.

**A**ccept all of your experiences without judgment or expectations.

**C**hoose: Respond to your experience and move forward.

We begin with chapter one—*Mindfulness Across the Lifespan*. Throughout your journey as you complete the readings and activities you will be reminded to practice mindfulness in all of your experiences. When you Mindfully Acknowledge your experience just as it is, pay Attention with all of your senses, thoughts, emotions and body, Accept your experience by letting go of judgments and expectations, and Choose how you show up for your experience—by responding versus reacting—you will engage in your life more fully.

Kheng Guan Toh/Shutterstock.com

Rawpixel.com/Shutterstock.com

Rene Jansa/Shutterstock.com

Rob Bayer/Shutterstock.com

Chapter two—*Developing a Mindful Ego: The Power of Emotional Intelligence*—discusses how we develop the tools enabling us to build confidence, set goals, build self-esteem and solidify emotional regulation. Through our developing years we increase our propensity for solid emotional intelligence when our relationships demonstrate love and acceptance without judgment and criticism. When we have emotional intelligence we are able to carve out the path to sustain living in the moment.

Chapter three, *The Positive Effects of Exercise Across the Lifespan* is a good reminder of how we begin life moving our limbs constantly before we can walk. If you stop for a moment to visualize a small baby you can see their arms and legs endlessly kicking and moving. Toddlers are like race horses taking off at the speed of lightening. Unfortunately as children and adults get older, the amount of activity often lessens. We develop habits where we are engaged in more sedentary activities resulting in obesity, diabetes, and other illness. These are not only the ills of adults but sadly children as well. Simply stated, we are born to move and move often. Let's get up and go!

Chapter four—*The Healing Power of Play, Laughter, and Humor*—is a reminder of how important the simple act of laughter, playing, and humor can be. When we laugh, an explosion of healing endorphins release. When we play, we can let go of restrictions and feel a sense of freedom. It is not unusual to find adults letting go when playing with children, allowing themselves to be silly, adventurous, and comical. The same may be found when adults play with animals. One may find themselves speaking in a higher-pitched voice, getting excited, participating in simple activities and games, singing without being self-conscious, and rolling on the floor with pleasure. As we mature and move along the lifespan, adults will find life more satisfying spending less time being serious and more time in the moment laughing and playing.

Chapter five—*Healthy Relationships Across the Lifespan*— is, without a doubt, the key to a satisfying life. Embracing each precious moment, connecting with others, feeling the touch of a warm hug, sharing feelings, helping each other when in need, enjoying companionship, and simply being in the presence of those who care is priceless. Taking the time to acknowledge each person in our lives just as they are, pay attention to them, embrace our time with them without judgment, and choose to be present for all of our experiences with them will undoubtedly increase intimacy, empathy and deepen our connection. When we let go of expectations we can truly enjoy our relationships without limitations.

Chapter six—*The Benefits of Connecting with Nature*— discusses the role nature plays in our lives. In our modern world of technology, things move quickly. We may overlook the beauty that nature provides, smelling the fragrance of a flower, being mesmerized watching a sunset, and reveling in the magic of watching trees and plants grow. Aside from the aesthetic aspects of nature, we receive a plethora of health benefits such as medicine from plants, vitamins from the sun, chlorophyll from greens grown in the garden, and oxygen delivered to our lungs, as well as the physical benefits of touching the earth while gardening, walking on the beach or on the grass. As you read through the chapter you will find that children and adults reap many healing benefits as they experience nature even in the simplest way.

Chapter Seven—*The Benefits of the Human-Animal Connection*—is not new news; yet, exploring how animals can enhance the quality of our lives is fascinating and noteworthy. Animals live mindfully, they are in the moment and totally present for all of their experiences. Our relationship with animals is different than our relationship with humans as animals have little expectations and are happy to simply enjoy our company just as we are. As you read through the chapter you will learn the many benefits to our mental and physical health as we connect with our animals. There is no limit as to how much love we can receive to improve our happiness. Remember to give your animal, if you have one, the attention they give you, forgive easily, and love unconditionally.

Chapter Eight—*Harmony Across the Lifespan: The Benefits of Music Throughout Our Lives*—discusses how we are influenced by music throughout our lives. Beginning at childhood, music impacts learning, as adult's music helps with relaxation, stress and pain reduction, and reflection. Music in general offers a pleasant experience whether listening at home, enjoying a concert or symphony, dancing, singing, or playing an instrument. Music, whether experienced alone or shared, is an activity we can all enjoy for all of our lives.

Chapter Nine—*The Artist Within Across the Lifespan*—offers you the opportunity to look inside yourself and witness your personal artist. We are all artists of one sort or another, whether our passion is a hobby, profession, or entertainment. You are guided to explore the artist within as a truth seeker, wisdom-bearer, and an artist who is not afraid to reach beyond the ordinary. We are all extraordinary in our own way and it is a gift to ourselves to look inside, step outside of our comfort zone of day-to-day living, and indulge in the challenge of who we are and can become.

Chapter Ten—*Happiness: Journey and Destination,* the final chapter, brings you to a peak of reflecting upon how happiness is crucial to your quality of life. As you move out of negative thinking and into developing a positive attitude and behaviors, you will begin to experience bliss and joy. Happy people have better health, practice gratitude, altruism, giving to others, forgive more, and are socially connected to others. If you stop and think about what contributes to your happiness, you might realize that time spent in activities that increase happiness are much more exciting than spending time that feed negativity.

*Whole Person Health: Mindful Living Across the Lifespan* walks you through looking through life's lens in ways that offer you new perspectives on how you decide to spend your time. Take time throughout your journey to explore your inner voice of creativity, whatever that may be—gardening, singing, strumming on the guitar, bird watching, painting for fun, experimenting with cooking, playing silly games with your pets or children. Allow yourself to move through time and whatever stage of life you are at, remember to create the space for listening to your inner voice of freedom, play, and exploration.

*Mindful Meditations: Reflections Across the Lifespan* offers you the opportunity to deepen your mindfulness practice. Practicing the three part breath and ocean breath gives you choices to practice breathing exercises. You have had many experiences in your life, some transforming and others ordinary. As you practice your mindful MAC meditations, each track will guide you to reflect upon your life from early childhood to the present time. When you read through the chapters and practice your mindful MAC meditations you will begin to see your life coming full circle.

Take a moment and fill out "My Whole Person Health" diagram below. Begin with 100% and designate how much of your time is spent in each life activity. Use the arrows to designate the percent. Do not forget to include how mindful you are. Are you satisfied, want to make changes, wondering how to add or eliminate certain activities? As you read through the chapters in *Whole Person Health: Mindful Living Across the Lifespan*, keep in mind what areas of your life you would like to develop.

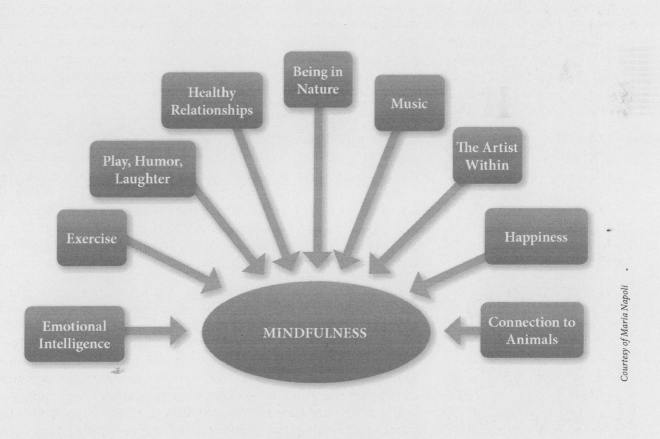

*Courtesy of Maria Napoli*

# CHAPTER 1

# Mindfulness Across the Lifespan

**Jamie Valderrama**

*Photo courtesy of Maria Napoli*

*Each moment matters*
*From beginning*
*to end*
*I am present*

Maria Napoli

*"Each morning we are born again. What we do today is what matters most."[1]*

Evgeny Atamanenko/Shutterstock.com

Acknowledging the breath, paying attention to the senses, accepting the experience without judgment, making a choice of whether you will respond or react to a situation…sound like therapy? In a way it is, and it is called mindfulness, a personal way to positively navigate the sometimes choppy waters of life via an ancient meditative practice designed to foster a state of being that engages in the moment without judgment.[2] Over the last three decades, mindfulness has been taught and implemented to children, teenagers, adults, parents, and students worldwide. A recent study evaluated a mindfulness-based social and emotional learning curriculum (MindUP) to see if it improved children's cognitive control, well-being, prosocial behavior, and academic performance.[3] The study concluded that the MindUP children showed significantly greater improvement in executive function reaction time. They also showed significant improvements on self-reported measures of empathy, perspective taking, optimism, emotional control, self-concept depressive symptoms, and mindfulness.[3] But it is not just with children that we are seeing such significant benefits. It is well known that mindfulness improves mood regulation in healthy adults (by looking at frontal EEG alpha wave asymmetry—higher left frontal alpha power is associated with depression, whereas higher right frontal alpha power is associated with approach motivation), but the data for depressed adults has been contradictory.[4] Fifty-seven women with a history of recurrent depressive disorder were induced to enter a sad mood and then applied either 20 minutes of mindful meditation or 20 minutes of a rumination challenge. The results showed an increase in right frontal alpha power for the mindful mediators with no benefit being showed for the ruminators; the conclusion is that mindfulness even helps those who are depressed.[4]

Mindfulness is even making its way into Congress with one politician, Tim Ryan, who recently wrote a book called *A Mindful Nation* that talks about his experience with mindfulness and how we can bring mindfulness more into our mainstream culture.[5] In recent years there have been numerous studies to show the varied benefits of mindfulness in general and more specifically throughout our lifetimes. In *The Mindful Brain*, Daniel Siegel, MD describes some of the following benefits of mindfulness.[6]

- **Body and emotion regulation:** When our bodies and emotions are balanced and appropriate in our lives.
- **Insight:** "Self-knowing awareness"—this is key to building positive social connections.
- **Attunement with others, i.e. "resonance":** This leads to the other person's experience of "feeling felt," of being understood. When children become more "tuned in" to themselves, they are more "tuned in" to others around them.
- **Empathy:** Allows us to see from the stance of another person's experience, imagining others' reality and perspective.
- **Better impulse control/response flexibility:** The capacity to pause before taking action (this is key with children and teens!); being able to consider a variety of possible options and to choose among them.

- **Fear modulation:** Our ability to calm and soothe, and even unlearn, our own fears.
- **Intuition:** Access to awareness of the wisdom of the body.
- **Increased attention span:** Practice of paying attention can build our attention muscles in our brains.
- **Morality:** Taking into consideration the larger picture; imagining and acting on what's best for the larger group rather than just ourselves.

This leads to the question—are you mindful or mind full? Do you live each day truly experiencing your story, focused on the interactions you have, while paying attention to the impact of the environment on your senses—allowing life to synergistically flow through you? Do you accept these moments authentically without judgment, understanding that they define the very foundation of your book, the words that create the sentences that eventually lead to the chapters of your life? Mindfulness is the pen with which we have the opportunity to write the story of our authentic lives, good and bad, pleasure and pain, without the cloud of judgment that so often blurs the edges and taints the font of our words. Ironically, we are born very mindful, a clear and concise text that only knows the moment; beginning chapters that clearly define who and what we are but as we progress, as all stories must, we become more complex, full of the past and the future. The simple clarity that started our story, the inherent mindfulness we were born with, soon becomes compromised as we actively lose our moment-to-moment existence to the complexities of maturity and our lives. To understand how this happens is to look at where it begins.

## ACTIVITY: MEANINGFUL QUOTE

What does the quote at the beginning of this chapter mean to you?

"Each morning we are born again. What we do today is what matters most."

_____

_____

_____

_____

_____

_____

_____

# Infancy Through Adolescence

*"The key to growth is the introduction of higher dimensions of consciousness into our awareness."[7]*

*Photosani/Shutterstock.com*

*Photo courtesy of Jamie Valderrama*

Babies and young children are inherently mindful and it all has to do with the brain. If we were to simplify the brain we could break it down into three major components: the reptilian (brainstem), mammalian (limbic), and thinking (neocortex) brain. The reptilian brain is responsible for instincts and autonomic responses (breathing, heart rate etc.), the mammalian for feelings and memory, and finally the neocortex for critical thinking, which encompasses all of our cognitive behavior.[8] The brains of babies and young children reflect this evolutionary development of the brain with the reptilian/brainstem being fully developed at birth, the mammalian/limbic brain following, and finally, at the end of adolescence into adulthood, the full development of the thinking/neocortex brain.[9] Therefore when a baby is hungry, a baby is hungry. There is no thought of a past meal nor a future meal—just a current meal. A baby automatically responds to the internal and external stimuli in its world without thought or judgment, is very much in the moment, and therefore is very mindful. We also see this with young children during play; the all-encompassing focus on the activity that they are engaged in, again without thought of future or past—only that moment, that activity on which they have directed all of their attention.

Unfortunately, that beautiful ability to be mindfully focused on that moment and the awareness of senses in that state start to change as a child's brain matures. With the maturation of the limbic and neocortex, a child starts becoming more aware of the emotions and feelings of those around them, relationships become more complex, and the awareness of how others view them becomes more important. Judgment becomes a shadow that hovers over internal and external actions and gone are the days of wearing princess dresses, superhero capes and dinosaur shoes. This new awareness ushers in insecurity, ruminations, and second guessing, which all undermine and pull away from the mindfulness that exists in as young children to the mindlessness that occurs as children begin moving into from middle childhood into adolescence.

There will never be such a dramatic change with the brain as there is from adolescence to young adulthood, aside from the development of the brain during infancy.[11] The limbic system is almost completely developed and the neocortex is closing the gap, but that gap is what gives teenagers their characteristic dramatic responses to life. It is because the limbic system is more mature at this point and the neocortex is still developing that teenagers feel with an intensity and depth that they will never experience again.[12] Once the neocortex (thinking center) matures, it will govern the emotional responses of the limbic system, curtailing the trademark rashness and sometimes illogical decisions that teenagers are known for, which inadvertently also pulls them away from mindfulness. Mindfulness is accepting that moment-to-moment experience without filters nor judgment and being a teenager is often all about judgment and insecurity and about not wanting to be in that moment. It is a period of time of moving from childhood to adulthood with a vehicle that is often not completely yet ready to make the journey.

"Teenagers. Everything is so apocalyptic."[10]

*David Pereiras/Shutterstock.com*

*vita khorzhevska/Shutterstock.com*

The amazing thing about mindfulness is that it can be introduced to children to help them navigate the rocky terrain of childhood and adolescence and we, as adult role models, have an immense responsibility to the young. It is in this journey from childhood to young adulthood that seeds can be planted and nurtured, providing a solid foundation from which our children can build a lifetime of mindfulness. One study showed that a family mindfulness program improved children's attention[13] while another study raises the distinct possibility that higher levels of maternal mindfulness may not only help expectant mothers reduce their anxiety, but may also benefit their children's auditory processing, thereby facilitating their speech and language development.[14]

Mindfulness interventions can improve the mental, emotional, social, and physical health and well-being of children. It has been shown to reduce stress, anxiety, reactivity, and bad behavior, improve sleep and self-esteem, and bring about greater calmness, relaxation, as well as the ability to manage behavior and emotions, self-awareness and empathy.[15] In addition to the physiological and psychological benefits of mindfulness, we see the positive effects carried over into the academic setting with studies showing increased executive function (ability to access the neocortex to increase problem solving, verbal abilities, attention and multi-tasking skills) in 7 to 9 year olds who participated in a mindfulness skills program as reported by their teachers and parents.[16] It is then critical that we look at the infrastructure we create for our children through home, school, and society with regards to the practice and implementation of mindfulness. It is through the interdisciplinary integration of these skills in childhood that the foundational building of mindfulness will be guided in adulthood.

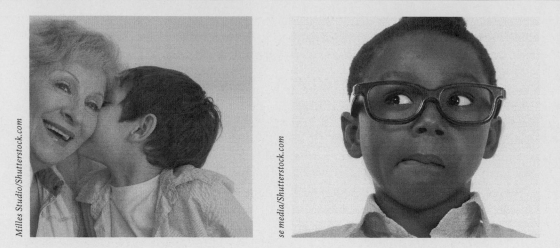

*Milles Studio/Shutterstock.com*

*se media/Shutterstock.com*

With the tremendous amount of research touting the benefits of mindfulness, how do you think mindfulness should be implemented in society for children?

_____

_____

_____

_____

_____

_____

_____

_____

_____

_____

_____

_____

_____

_____

_____

# Adulthood

*"For in every adult there dwells the child that was, and in every child there lies the adult that will be."*[17]

*Rob Marmion/Shutterstock.com*

*Blend Images/Shutterstock.com*

*Blend Images/Shutterstock.com*

Erikson's psychosocial stages of adulthood are categorized in three stages; Young (19–40 years old), Middle (40–65 years old) and Mature (65 years old to death). It is here that we both create and reap the type of mindful life we currently have and want to create for the future. We are now making our own decisions on careers, partners, children, and the personal activities we pursue. It is a time of tremendous change and with that change can come stress, the sympathetic response that pulls us away from mindfulness.

To look at stress more closely is to look at the nervous system. The nervous system can be broken down into the central nervous system (brain and spinal cord) and peripheral nervous system (everything else), which then branches to the autonomic nervous system and somatic nervous system. The somatic nervous system controls all of our voluntary responses (such as picking this book up to read), while our autonomic nervous system controls our involuntary responses (heart rate, respiration, hormones).

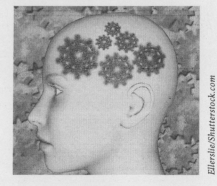

*Ellerslie/Shutterstock.com*

When we are perceiving a real or imagined threat, the nervous system will activate the autonomic nervous system and prepare the body for flight, fight, or freeze. When this occurs, the immune and digestive systems are subdued and the brain also adjusts, disengaging the neocortex and engaging the limbic and brainstem—physiologically, you are incapable of being mindful in this moment; it is purely about maintaining the integrity of the organism and escaping the threat (real or perceived). When the stressor is gone, then the body returns to homeostatsis. The parasympathetic nervous system then is the antithesis of sympathetic. When we are in the parasympathetic nervous system (rest and digest), all of our systems are working (immune and digestive) and all three sections of our brain (reptilian, mammalian, and neocortex) are in sync.[18]

Mindfulness is key in balancing these three sections. It is through the act of being present and acknowledging the situation without judgment that we are able to sync the brain. This is not to undermine the importance of the sympathetic nervous system, which is vital to our survival. We have it to ensure survival of the human organism in times of danger; unfortunately in today's world we are facing less

4 Step **MAC** Guide
Mindfully
acknowledge
attention
accept
choose

real external stimuli that is actually capable of harming us and more perceived internal stimuli (job loss, family stress, relationships).

It is at this time in our lives that the cultivation of mindful activities we have practiced and continue to implement is paramount to the happiness we will have as we move through adulthood. The ability to recognize our movement into the sympathetic system is the ability to learn to respond versus react to potential stimuli (both internal and external). In many ways, the ability to be mindful, to respond versus react to stress, is reflective of an old Cherokee Indian story.

## The Two Wolves: A Cherokee Story

*Jozef Klopacka/Shutterstock.com*

It is at this time in our lives that the cultivation of mindful activities we have practiced and continue to implement is paramount to the happiness we will have as we move through adulthood. The ability to recognize our movement into the sympathetic system is the ability to learn to respond versus react to potential stimuli (both internal and external). In many ways, the ability to be mindful, to respond versus react to stress, is reflective of an old Cherokee Indian story.

One evening, an elderly
Cherokee brave told his
grandson about a battle that
goes on inside people.

He said "My son, the battle is
between two 'wolves' inside us all.
One is evil. It is anger,
envy, jealousy, sorrow,
regret, greed, arrogance,
self-pity, guilt, resentment,
inferiority, lies, false pride,
superiority, and ego.

The other is good.
It is joy, peace love, hope serenity,
humility, kindness, benevolence,
empathy, generosity,
truth, compassion, and faith."

The grandson though about
it for a minute and then asked
his grandfather:

"Which wolf wins?"

The old Cherokee simply replied,
"The one that you feed."[19]

Author Unknown

The message within this story applies to mindfulness in that when we are faced with a stressful situation we have a choice as to whether we will mindfully respond versus react. Do we allow (feed) the sympathetic nervous system to engage when a perceived threat looms on the horizon or do we choose to stay (feed) in the parasympathetic nervous system where we know we are allowing our immune system, digestion, and sleep patterns to be maximized? One clinical trial showed that mindfulness training in adults 55 years and older improved sleep[20] while another shows the restoration of self control over aggressive behavior.[21]

Applied mindfulness gives us the power to control the sympathetic response through the deliberate re-engagement of the neocortex. When we are being mindful, we are thoughtfully (thinking) acknowledging the situation, paying attention to our senses, choosing what action we will take, and above all else not judging it.[22] A study involving the release of cortisol (a known stress hormone) in women showed that mindfulness traits protected stress-related increases in cortisol after waking up in the morning.[23] To top off all of the benefits already stated, the findings of one study suggests that meditation may slow normal brain atrophy associated with aging,[24] a perk that in an ever-increasing older adult cohort we cannot ignore.

## ACTIVITY: REAL VERSUS PERCEIVED STRESS

Kues/Shutterstock.com

1. Give examples of a real and a perceived stress that you have experienced in your life.

_____

_____

_____

_____

_____

_____

_____

2. When authentically looking at your life, which wolves are you choosing to feed?

_____

_____

_____

_____

_____

_____

_____

# Mindful Activities for Everyone

*"Science and mindfulness complement each other in helping people to eat well and maintain their health and well-being."*[25]

Vitalinka/Shutterstock.com

Mindfulness can be practiced at any time, in any place and at any age. To practice mindfulness is to pay attention, non-judgmentally accept, and move forward with positive intentions. Therefore, mindfulness activities can be manipulated and implemented to fit the individual, fitness level, and age of all individuals. Whether it is for a child of 3 or an adult of 103, mindfulness can effortlessly be incorporated in all aspects of life. The following mindful activities have been pulled from *Tools for Mindful Living*[26] and *Life by Personal Design*[22]—books that are part of a stress management program taught to both undergraduate and graduate students at Arizona State University.

The classes focus on mindfulness by implementing a four-step MAC Mindfulness Model to be applied to different activities by (1) emphatically acknowledging each experience; (2) intentionally paying attention to your senses, thoughts, emotions, and instincts regarding each experience; (3) accepting your experience without judgment or internal or external filters; and (4) choosing to respond or react to your present experience.

# Mindfully Breathing

*"Remember to breathe. It is after all, the secret of life."*[27]

Mindful breathing refers to diaphragmatic breathing that engages both the chest and stomach (the diaphragm is the muscle that separates these two cavities). It is the deep belly breath that we see naturally when a young child sleeps; the whole body moves, bringing in oxygen through inhalation and carbon dioxide through exhalation. It is the quickest way to bring the body from sympathetic (flight/flight) to parasympathetic (rest/digest) and it can be done anywhere and at any time.

racorn/Shutterstock.com

- Find a position that is comfortable, either sitting or lying down. (Make sure that the diaphragm is not compressed.)
- Place your hands on your stomach so that you can feel it rise like a balloon as you inhale (bring breath in) and exhale (letting the breath out).
- Inhale for a count of 10…hold for a count of 10…exhale for a count of 10.
- Pay attention to the breath as you inhale and exhale. How do you feel? What are your senses telling you?
- Continue for as long as you like. Any amount of time in this activity is beneficial.

# Mindfully Breathing

*"One should eat to live, not live to eat."*[28]

We are a society that is in the midst of an obesity epidemic. We have more accessibility to food, both healthy and unhealthy, and limited time in which to eat it. More and more people are eating either on the go (in cars, walking to school, public transport) or in front of technology (TV, computers, and cell phones), leading to mindless eating habits that are contributing to our current obesity epidemic. Mindful eating is not just a healthy way to approach food, but a crucial way to help change our relationship with food.

- For one week eat one meal per day in silence.
- Notice the food in front of you (e.g., color, smells, and textures).
- Sit in a comfortable chair and clear your eating space of any distractions: technology, magazines, work, and so forth.

- Notice the food with your eyes as you bring the food towards your mouth.
- Savor the smells of the food.
- Chew your food 25 to 50 times before swallowing.
- Listen to the sounds of your chewing and notice the sensations in your mouth.

## Mindful Walking

*"Walking is man's best medicine."*[29]

In our busy lives we do not often take advantage of the opportunities to take a walk just for the purpose of taking a walk. We have schedules and agendas and want to get from point A to point B as quickly as we can. In the process, we focus on our phones or music and do not truly pay attention to the environment or people around us. Mindfully walking is a wonderful way to not only connect internally but with nature and the ones you love.

David Pereiras/Shutterstock.com

- For one week take a walk for 15 minutes a day.
- Scan the feelings in your body front and back from head to toe while walking.
- Notice what your body is communicating.
- Pay attention to your surroundings. Remember it is not about the destination but the journey.
- What are your senses telling you? What do you see, hear, smell, and feel on your skin?
- Touch a flower, branch, or blade of grass and focus on the texture.

## Mindful Communication

*"Whatever words we utter should be chosen with care for people will hear them and be influenced by them for good or ill."*[30]

Think about the last person you spoke to today. When they were talking to you, were you already forming a response in your head? If you were, as many of us do, then we can say that you were not mindfully listening. How about attention. Were you fully invested in the conversation you were having? Did you fully acknowledge the person you were speaking with by maintaining eye contact and thoughtfully responding or were you checking your phone, your computer, or thinking

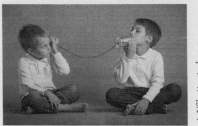

pio3/Shutterstock.com

about another task? Many times we believe we are mindfully engaged with the people in our lives when in fact we are mindlessly engaged. Here are a few tips to ensure everyone you interact with knows that you value and respect what they have to say.

4 Step MAC Guide
Mindfully
acknowledge
attention
accept
choose

- Acknowledge your companion by paraphrasing what they said; use your own words to ensure you received their information.
- Pay attention to your companion's behavior to clarify what you feel and hear.
- Before you offer feedback, wait until your companion is finished speaking; then give your thoughts, opinions, and feelings without judgment.
- When responding, own your experience and make "I" statements; we take responsibility for our actions, words, and behavior, enhancing our ability to mindfully communicate.

## ACTIVITY: INCORPORATING MINDFULNESS

Rido/Shutterstock.com

1. How do you think you could incorporate diaphragmatic breathing into your life?

_____

_____

_____

_____

2. Explain how mindfully eating may correlate to fighting the obesity epidemic.

_____

_____

_____

_____

3.  Where could you take a mindful walk in your neighborhood and with whom would you want to share it?

_____

_____

_____

_____

4.  How could more mindful conversations benefit relationships?

_____

_____

_____

_____

# References

1.  Kornfield, J. (1994). *Buddha's little instruction book* (p. 79). New York: Bantam Books.

2.  Arkowitz, H., & Lilienfeld, S. (2014). Is mindfulness good medicine? *Scientific American Mind*, *25*(5), 74–75.

3.  Schonert-Reichl, K. A., Oberle, E., Lawlor, M. S., Abbott, D., Thomson, K., Oberlander, T. F., & Diamond, A. (2015). Enhancing cognitive and social-emotional development through a simple-to-administer mindfulness-based school program for elementary school children: A randomized controlled trial. *Developmental Psychology. 51*(1), 52.

4.  Keune, P. M., Bostanov, V., Hautzinger, M., & Kotchoubey, B. (2013). Approaching dysphoric mood: State-effects of mindfulness meditation on frontal brain asymmetry. *Biological Psychology, 93(1)*, 105–13. [PMID: 23410762]

5.  Ryan, T. (2012). *A mindful nation: How a simple practice can help us reduce stress, improve performance, and recapture the American spirit.* Carlsbad, CA: Hay House.

6.  Siegal, D. (2007). *The mindful brain: Reflection and attunement in the cultivation of well-being.* New York: W.W. Norton & Company.

7.  Lao Tzu. (n.d.). BrainyQuote.com. Retrieved August 30, 2015 from http://www.brainyquote.com/quotes/quotes/l/laotzu118184.html

8. Seaward, B. (2009). Physiology of stress. In *Managing stress: Principles and strategies for health and well-being* (6th ed., pp. 37–39). Sudbury, MA: Jones and Bartlett.

9. Williamson, N., & Mitchell, A. (2013, January 1). Early brain development: Policy makes a difference. Retrieved March 1, 2015 from http://www.bbbgeorgia.org/docs/Early Brain Development - Policy Makes a Difference.pdf

10. Garcia, K., Stohl, M., & Little, B. (2009). *Beautiful creatures*. New York: Little, Brown.

11. Supekar, K., Musen, M., & Menon, V. (2009). Development of large-scale functional brain networks in children. *PLOS: Biology, 1000157*. Retrieved March 1, 2015 from http://journals.plos.org/plosbiology/article?id=10.1371/journal.pbio.1000157

12. Friedman, R. (2014, June 28). Why teenagers act crazy. *The New York Times.* Retrieved March 1, 2015 from http://www.nytimes.com/2014/06/29/opinion/sunday/why-teenagers-act-crazy.html?_r=0

13. Felver, J. C., Tipsord, J. M., Morris, M. J., Racer, K. H., & Dishion, T. J. (2014). The effects of mindfulness-based intervention on children's attention regulation. *Journal of Attention Disorders.* Aug 29. pii: 1087054714548032.

14. van den Heuvel, M. I., Donkers, F. C., Winkler, I., Otte, R. A., & Van den Bergh, B. R. (2014). Maternal mindfulness and anxiety during pregnancy affect infants' neural responses to sounds. *Social Cognitive and Affective Neuroscience. 10*(3), 453–460.

15. Weare, K. (2012). Evidence for the impact of mindfulness on children and young people. *The Mindfulness in Schools Project.* Retrieved March 1, 2015 from http://mindfulnessinschools.org/wp-content/uploads/2013/02/MiSP-Research-Summary-2012.pdf

16. Flook, L., Smalley, S.L., Kitil, M.J., Galla, B.M., Kaiser-Greenland, S., Locke, J., Ishijima, E., & Kasari, C. (2010). Effects of mindful awareness practices on executive functions in elementary school children. *Journal of Applied School Psychology, 26*(1), 70–95.

17. Connolly, J. (2006). *The book of lost things*. New York: Atria Books.

18. Bercelli, D. (2008). *The revolutionary trauma release process*. Vancouver, BC: Namaste Publishing.

19. Tale of Two Wolves. Retrieved March 1, 2015 from http://www.nanticokeindians.org/tale_of_two_wolves.cfm

20. Black, D. S., O'Reilly, G. A., Olmstead, R., Breen, E. C., & Irwin, M. R. (2015). Mindfulness meditation and improvement in sleep quality and daytime impairment among older adults with sleep disturbances: A randomized clinical trial. *JAMA Internal Medicine. 175*(4), 494–501.

21. Yusainy, C., & Lawrence, C. (2015). Brief mindfulness induction could reduce aggression after depletion. *Consciousness and Cognition, 33*, 125–134.

22. Napoli, M., & Roe, S. (2011). *Life by personal design* (2nd ed.). Dubuque, IA: Kendall Hunt.

23. Daubenmier, J., Hayden, D., Chang, V., & Epel, E. (2014). It's not what you think: Dispositional mindfulness moderates the relationship between psychological distress and the cortisol awakening response. *Psychoneuroendocrinology, 48*:11–18. [PMID: 24971591]

24. Luders, E., Cherbuin, N., & Kurth, F. (2014). Forever young (er): Potential age-defying effects of long-term meditation on gray matter atrophy. *Frontiers in Psychology*, 5, 1551.

25. Nhat Hanh. (n.d.). BrainyQuote.com. Retrieved August 30, 2015, from http://www.brainyquote.com/quotes/quotes/n/nhathanh591371.html

26. Napoli, M. (2011). *Tools for mindful living* (2nd ed.). Dubuque, IA: Kendall Hunt.

27. Maguire, G. (2008). *A lion among men*. New York: William Morrow.

28. Moliere. (n.d.). BrainyQuote.com. Retrieved August 30, 2015 from http://www.brainyquote.com/quotes/quotes/m/moliere138703.html

29. Hippocrates. (n.d.). BrainyQuote.com. Retrieved August 30, 2015 from http://www.brainyquote.com/quotes/quotes/h/hippocrate380084.html

30. Buddha. (n.d.). BrainyQuote.com. Retrieved August 30, 2015 from http://www.brainyquote.com/quotes/quotes/b/buddha118669.html

## CHAPTER 1 QUESTIONS

1. How long has mindfulness been around and what does it mean to be mindful?

2. What are five benefits of mindfulness and how do they positively affect behavior?

    1)

    2)

    3)

    4)

    5)

3. What are the three major areas of the brain and how do they develop in a baby's brain?

4. Why are teenagers so emotional?

5. How does mindfulness help children?

6. Why does the sympathetic response take us away from mindfulness?

7. How does mindfulness help re-engage the parasympathetic nervous system?

8. What are some benefits of mindfulness for adults?

9. What is diaphragmatic breathing?

10. What is the difference between mindfully eating a meal versus the normal way we eat?

# MINDFUL AWARENESS REFLECTION JOURNAL

4 Step **MAC** Guide

Choose one mindful experience as you begin your reflection.

### Empathically Acknowledge

Describe your experience.

_____

_____

_____

### Intentional Attention

Describe what you noticed.

| |
|---|
| Breath |
| Body |
| Emotions |
| Thoughts |
| Senses |

### Accept Without Judgment

Describe judgment; acceptance.

_____

_____

_____

### Willingly Choose

Choose to purposely respond to your experience.

_____

_____

_____

### Mindful Mac Meditation

Describe your meditation experiences. What did you learn from your meditation experience?

_____

_____

_____

# Mindful Daily Journal

_____
_____
_____
_____

_____
_____
_____
_____
_____
_____
_____
_____
_____
_____
_____
_____
_____
_____

*Tips for Wellbeing*

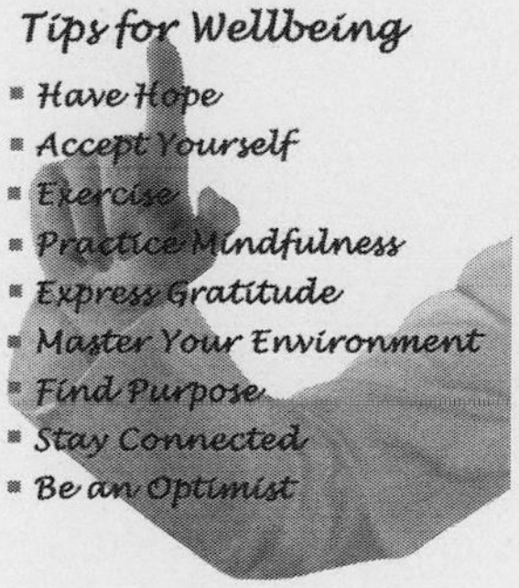

- Have Hope
- Accept Yourself
- Exercise
- Practice Mindfulness
- Express Gratitude
- Master Your Environment
- Find Purpose
- Stay Connected
- Be an Optimist

_____
_____
_____
_____

Date: _____ Make Today Count!

# Developing a Mindful Ego: The Power of Emotional Intelligence

**Steve Peterson**

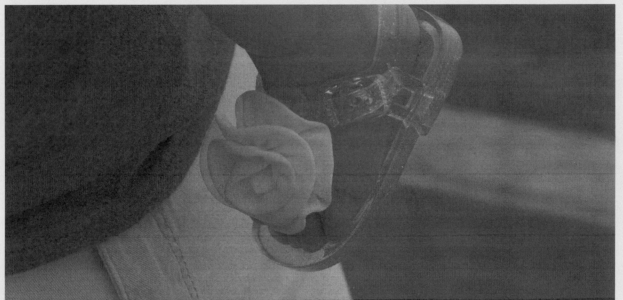

*Photo courtesy of Maria Napoli*

*There is no greater gift than to be loved*

*Receiving love naturally opens the door to giving love*

*How beautiful life can be*

Maria Napoli

Sergey Nivens/Shutterstock.com

There is often a negative social connotation associated with the word ego.

*"Well THAT person sure does have a big ego!"*

*"Walk behind him because his EGO has to fit through the door first!"*

We tend to associate ego with a personal superiority complex or inflated sense of self-esteem. There is a sense of judgment that we often pass onto the reference of someone's ego and compartmentalize that judgment into a place that we do not necessarily want to visit. We may label it as an unpleasant personality trait and disassociate ourselves from that person. Often overlooked is the presence of *low* or *undeveloped ego* strength, which may result in a lack of confidence in one's personality, thinking and motive in life; herein lies the possibility for long-term self-esteem issues, depression, and failure to connect and develop positive and healthy relationships.

It is unfortunate that the term *ego* has been misrepresented, and its true personal development value underestimated. Its role in our overall health and mental well-being is often seriously underrepresented. It is important that ego development be seen for what its true purpose is and that it is understood that one is not born with their ego intact: it is a learned and developed characteristic of the psyche that can be easily modified and brought into a healthy state of being.

How do we define ego? Ego is the organized mediator between the person and their perception of, and adaptation to, reality. The ego is responsible for reality testing and one's sense of personal identity.[2]   The ego is molded and groomed by our emotional responses (tacit and explicit) to social-environmental events we are exposed to. I like to think of it as the psychological coping mechanism to situations and events that manifests itself as a physiological reaction. Most often at the root of an unhealthy ego (unusually high or excessively low) are unresolved emotional issues.[3]

Photo courtesy of Maria Napoli

Let's dial in on the ego, understand how it is developed, respect its role in our daily lives, and learn how to align it for health and happiness. Take a moment and follow this story.

Baby John is born. Aside from his basic reflexive capabilities such as breathing, most of his needs are met by his caretakers. He does not have any filters of what is good or bad; he only knows what he wants when he wants it. If his needs are successfully met, John learns that the world is a safe place. As he gets a bit older, he navigates away from his caretakers and experiments with meeting his own needs, feeding himself, feeling a sense of accomplishment when completing a puzzle, and receiving a loving hug when he kisses his caretaker. What is happening to John is the development of emotional intelligence. He is learning how to negotiate his environment and respond to or react to experiences. The most significant factor here is how John's experiences move him toward a healthy ego development through receiving consistent positive feedback and reinforcement throughout his developing years. As a result of these positive responses, John is able to deal with both negative and positive emotions, thoughts and experiences. He has developed good Emotional Intelligence.

On the other hand, if John's experiences have been inconsistent, negative, and worst of all, abusive or negligent, his ability to manage his emotions, thoughts, and experiences will most likely be erratic and reactive.

Let's look at a few examples throughout different stages of the lifespan of how the disconnect between psychological coping and physiological reaction (an unhealthy ego) can play a *part* in certain behaviors.

- Bullying: Outward harassment and belittling of another denoting repressed feelings of insecurity and lack of a healthy interactive social acceptance.[4]
- Abusive relationships: Anger and physical/emotional torment stemming from lack of personal control and failure in nurturing past relationships. On the part of the victim, blind acceptance and making excuses because of low self-esteem, feelings of guilt and fear of being alone.[5]
- Elderly depression: Feelings of loneliness and lack of self-worth because of personal social changes and fear of death.[6]

The manifestation of an unhealthy ego arises when our emotions direct and manipulate its ability to provide a healthy response.

For one's health and wellness, it is important to redefine the social construct of ego and begin developing it into a *mindful ego*. Developing a mindful ego is accomplished by harnessing our emotions in a responsive, not reactive, way.

## ACTIVITY: EGO IDENTIFICATION

*"The ultimate aim of the ego is not to see something, but to be something."*

—Muhammad Iqbal[7]

Select three people you feel possess an unhealthy ego. Perhaps one of those people is you.

Describe the way they react in certain situations and then identify what you feel is the ego-driven root cause of these reactions. Follow the 4 Step MAC Guide to assist you in harnessing harmony in how you are better able to respond to your experiences versus reacting to them.

Person #1: _____

| How they react | Ego-driven root cause |
| --- | --- |
|  |  |

Person #2: _____

| How they react | Ego-driven root cause |
| --- | --- |
|  |  |

Person #3: _____

| How they react | Ego-driven root cause |
| --- | --- |
|  |  |

## What Is a *Mindful Ego*?

A mindful ego employs the strategies of mindfulness to restructure the emotional impact on our ego. It essentially requires the employment of basic tenets of mindfulness in our daily lives to affect our

psychological coping mechanisms; hence, resulting in a proactive, positive response to potential stressors and perceptions to reality that ultimately elicits our responses toward ourselves and others. Be genuine and honest with yourself. Only then can you be genuine and honest with others. Mindfulness-based stress reduction (MBSR) is a practice that has been employed for over the past two decades to assist healthy individuals improve their coping abilities with the stresses of daily life.[8] Mindful awareness is neither esoteric nor religious in nature; rather it is a "dispassionate, nonevaluative and sustained moment-to-moment awareness"[9] of a perceived mental state. It is nondeliberative and pulls one away from the daily "autopilot" of social-behavioral interaction. For the individual, a mindful ego affords a more accurate perception of one's own mental responses to stimuli (both internal and external) and leads to a more prominent sense of control.

Put into practice, every day and with everybody, these thirteen basic tenets:

- Be in the here and now. Not yesterday. Not tomorrow.
- Practice nonjudgmental acceptance. Of yourself. And others.
- Pay attention. To the small, unexciting details of everyday experience and interaction.
- Have a clear conscience. It's over. Move on.
- If you are feeling depressed, you are living in the past. If you are anxious, you are living in the future. If you are at peace, you are living in the present.
- Focus all of your attention in the present moment.
- Have clarity and focus in your immediate task at hand. Try not to multitask.
- Avoid vanity in yourself and criticism of others.
- Laugh and cry and dance and mope around as if no one cares.
- Love unconditionally.
- Forgive without looking back. Yourself and others.
- Minimize your expectations of others. Appreciate worth for worth sake.

It can be argued that a high level of self-esteem (positive ego) presents a greater level of personal health and efficaciousness than a disproportionately low level of self-esteem. But all too often either spectrum of self-esteem remains untethered by a level of mindfulness. Individuals that practice and present an elevated level of mindfulness possess an elevated level of self-esteem that is secure rather than fragile.[10] Fragile levels of self-esteem are indicated by unusually high or excessively low egos, as they are directed by a lack of emotional control.

A mindful ego puts oneself *first* in the moment of personal solitude, yet affords others undivided and nonjudgmental attention *first* when in their company, a disciplined level of intrinsic and extrinsic control and so easy to accomplish!

## How Do I Develop My *Mindful Ego?*

This is very simple. You develop your mindful ego by harnessing your *emotional intelligence!*

Yes, you have an emotional intelligence. It has never been measured. You can't take a standardized test to assign a numerical value to it and compare it to a standard statistical deviation. It won't get you into Harvard University if you do poorly on your SATs.

There are seven tools used to measure the human intelligence quotient (IQ), or more recently referred to as the "deviation IQ." The Wechsler Intelligence Scales, Stanford-Binet Intelligence Scale, Woodcock-Johnson Test of

Bork/Shutterstock.com

Cognitive Abilities, Kaufman Tests, Cognitive Assessment System, Differential Ability Scales and the Reynolds Intellectual Ability Scales. It is commonly held that intelligence quotient tests administered at an early age are generally a reliable predictor of lifelong IQ scores.[11]

Although subject to scrutiny and academic challenge, let's just hold onto that broad brushstroke statement for a moment.

If it is safe to assume that most of us maintain a relatively stable level of measurable intelligence throughout the course of our lives; that means we cannot radically change our level of intelligence simply by waking up one Thursday morning, deciding we want a new IQ, and start doing something about it, and BOOM! by Sunday we are more intelligent! Wouldn't that be nice! Sorry, this is not going to happen. What we CAN change in the matter of a few days is our emotional intelligence (often referred to as EI or EQ—emotion quotient).

Emotional intelligence is, by standardized testing modalities, an immeasurable and personally-developed cognitive ability to evaluate, control, and perceive emotions. Peter Salovey and John D. Mayer defined emotional intelligence as "a subset of social intelligence that involves the ability to monitor one's own and others' feelings and emotions, to discriminate among them and to use this information to guide one's thinking and actions."[12]

The very nature of a lack of a standard measurable medium indicates that emotional intelligence is a fluid cognitive construct that is adaptive, can be developed, and can be changed over time, unlike the conventionally-held position of the intelligent quotient. We have the ability and capability to strengthen our emotional intelligence and, in the process, develop a healthy mindful ego!

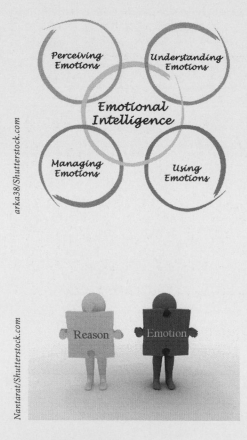

arka38/Shutterstock.com

Nantaral/Shutterstock.com

There is a model, as proposed by Salovey and Mayer, that identifies four factors of emotional intelligence: perceiving emotions, reasoning with emotions, understanding emotions, and managing emotions.[12]

*Perceiving emotions* is the first step in understanding and processing emotions. Here we are referring to perception not only of others, but also of our own emotions. This begins by picking up on nonverbal cues such as facial expressions, body language, and personal communicating mannerisms.

Remember, emotional perception is just as applicable to ourselves when *we* are attempting to mindfully monitor our present experience, so don't be afraid to glance in a mirror, and definitely pay attention to your own reflection in public spaces. You can learn just as much by paying attention to the subtleties of yourself just as you can in others.

Mindfulness begins with you. Only after you can be comfortably mindful with yourself can you be effectively mindful toward others.

*Reasoning with emotions* is, in effect, prioritizing what we pay attention to. We tend to respond to things that grab our emotional attention. The key is to allow ourselves to *respond to* instead of *react to* those events regardless of the positive or negative emotion that we are experiencing. Understanding that responding to emotions instead of reacting is of paramount importance in practicing mindfulness. Remember, all of our emotions are important; it is how we are mindful in expressing them that makes a difference. It is a fundamental premise of stress management. Therefore, when encountering a potentially stressful event, ask yourself:

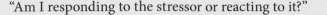

4 Step MAC Guide
Mindfully
acknowledge
attention
accept
choose

"Am I responding to the stressor or reacting to it?"

*Understanding emotions* calls upon a mindful interpretation of what is really occurring whether within yourself or when interacting with someone else. When someone has experienced a positive, happy, or exciting event, they tend to immediately want to share that with others. If you were to ask them why they are so happy, they can often give you an immediate and concise answer. Positive emotions tend to remove judgmental opinions and frequently make people very approachable, allowing for clear and concise thought processes. There are two chemicals responsible for this response: endorphins and dopamine.

Endorphins are neurotransmitters that act upon the opiate receptors in the brain to reduce our perception of pain and cause a "euphoric" emotional state.[13]

Dopamine is both a hormone (released when the body is in parasympathetic mode) and a neurotransmitter. Dopamine provides us with a feeling of enjoyment and acts as a motivator to continue to pursue said feelings of enjoyment.[14]

By contrast, it is incredibly difficult to "pin down" exactly what the root cause is of negative emotion or anger. For example, if a supervisor exhibits anger or hostility toward a subordinate, can you explain why simply by observing?

Compare that to someone who is holding a soft, snuggling puppy. They have a big smile on their face and their eyes are lit up. By simply observing can you explain why that person is happy? Precisely. On the other hand when trying to answer why the supervisor is demonstrating anger/hostility, we are unable to identify the root cause because there are many possibilities:

The subordinate may be a poor worker and dropped an expensive piece of equipment.

Or the supervisor received a speeding ticket on the way in to work that morning.

Or the supervisor is having a fight with his/her significant other.

Or the supervisor had their vehicle stolen the night before.

*maxim ibragimov/Shutterstock.com*

*Leonid Andronov/Shutterstock.com*

DOPAMINE

*Zerbor/Shutterstock.com*

Or it could be this.

Or it could be that.

Or the supervisor could just be a mean-spirited person.

There are a myriad of possibilities.

See what I am getting at? Positive emotions are often identifiable and easy to perceive, reason with, and understand, where negative emotions are often not.

Negative emotions often elicit anxiety, which may inhibit our inability to cognitively discern these emotions. Anxiety and stressful events put our bodies in a reactive mode and causes the release of other neurotransmitters, adrenaline, and cortisol. During these periods we may become unapproachable, lack those clear and concise thought processes, and react in a very judgmental and blaming way. All mindfulness is "out the window" at this point.

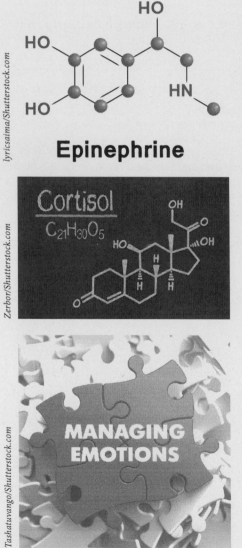

*lyricsaima/Shutterstock.com*

**Epinephrine**

*Zerbor/Shutterstock.com*

*Tashatuvango/Shutterstock.com*

*Bob Alex/Shutterstock.com*

The two chemicals responsible for this phenomenon are epinephrine and cortisol.

Epinephrine (known as adrenaline) also carries the role of hormone and neurotransmitter. Unlike dopamine, epinephrine keeps the body in the "fight or flight response." This is the sympathetic response mode of self-preservation during times of physiological duress.[15]

Cortisol is a hormone that acts as the body's natural "anti-inflammatory" chemical. Cortisol is a fast-acting chemical that is released in preparation for tissue damage and in response to a physical trauma.[16] There is a lesson to be learned from this: positive emotions and negative emotions cannot function at the same time. The body cannot be in sympathetic mode and parasympathetic modes at the same time. The hormones and neurotransmitters mentioned previously fundamentally act to balance the body, which means the two groups operate independently of each other.

The key to discerning the two is having a mindful approach to responding…not reacting…to emotions. Yours. And others.

The final component of the model is *managing emotions*.

This is perhaps the crux of emotional intelligence. It is important to have a mindful approach to perception, reasoning, and understanding of emotions in order to effectively manage your response to them. In the regulation of one's own response and determining the appropriate response, not reaction, to what is often overlooked is our fundamental desire to multi-task, because we are often so busy. Mindfulness requires a strict absence of multi-tasking. One must be in the moment and pay strict attention to the emotion at hand, not focusing on anything else.

Take a moment and practice your mindful ego on yourself. Invoke your emotional intelligence as a "self-diagnostic" exercise.

Do this by backing into the question of whether you are happy or not.

Ask yourself responsive diagnostic questions.

- Am I feeling social?
- Are my thoughts clear?
- Can I clearly and concisely articulate what is making me feel what I'm feeling now?

If you can answer affirmatively, then you are in a positive state of emotion. You have mindfully recognized your own ego.

If you cannot, then you know what needs to change. Turn off the sympathetic reactive mode and put yourself into a parasympathetic response state of mind.

Mindfulness is growth. And growth is change. And change can be scary. It is scary because it is not something we are necessarily accustomed to and requires personal effort.

If you really think about it, change can be quite reactionary. Reaction often stems from an event or experience that did not play out the way we expected. It may have caused us some personal duress. It was a stressor. Or…in this particular case that I am trying to present to you…it is something that you have never thought about. It is new. It is uncharted waters.

Which means it might be scary for you. But that is all right. Because, as Jack Canfield once stated, "Everything you want is on the other side of fear."

In order to effectively realize our mindful selves and embrace our emotional intelligence, we need to integrate that fear, not necessarily give power to that fear, but identify it as a source of emotional dissonance and make the mindful determination to manipulate it into a responsive emotional outcome; instead of allowing that fear to make us bitter, we are going to move into the fear and then let it go!

There is no shame in acknowledging that we have fear, negative emotions, and pain. The key is to accept them as very human experiences and be done with them, never allowing them to have power over our new-found emotional intelligence.

## **ACTIVITY:** EGO IDENTIFICATION PART TWO

*"Men are not prisoners of fate, but prisoners of their own minds."*

—Franklin D. Roosevelt[17]

Refer back to the three people you identified earlier as possessing an unhealthy ego.

Except this time, articulate how each person could better *respond* instead of *react* to the ego-driven root cause.

Person #1: _____

| Ego-driven root cause | A mindful ego response would be... |
|---|---|
|  |  |

Person #2: _____

| Ego-driven root cause | A mindful ego response would be... |
|---|---|
|  |  |

Person #3: _____

| Ego-driven root cause | A mindful ego response would be... |
|---|---|
|  |  |

# Activity: Brain Versus Mind

*"Our minds influence the key activity of the brain, which then influences everything; perception, cognition, thoughts and feelings, personal relationships; they're all a projection of you."*

—Deepak Chopra[18]

Explain your understanding of the difference between the brain and the mind:

_____

_____

_____

_____

_____

_____

_____

_____

_____

_____

_____

_____

_____

_____

_____

_____

_____

_____

Naeblys/Shutterstock.com

patrice6000/Shutterstock.com

Do something today that your future self will thank you for.

Wiktoria Pawlak/Shutterstock.com

Let's differentiate between the brain and the mind.

Everyone knows where their brain is. The brain has a fixed position in the body, can be removed, and examined. There is no doubt what the brain looks like; it is scientifically measurable and can be medically modified.

But where is the mind? What does it look like? Where is it? Can you hold it? Measure it?

Therein lies the greatest fascination and power of the mind. Unlike the brain that is fueled by blood at its core and electrical connections throughout the grey matter, the mind is a bit more ethereal and is fueled by experiences and interpretations and memories that guide the brain to carry out certain physiological functions.

The brain is composed of nerve cells and blood vessels. It is an organ, the center of the nervous system, and is responsible for coordinating movements and carrying out thoughts and expressing feelings.

The brain requires no input from us for it to carry out rudimentary and reflexive events such as breathing, heartbeat, and blinking.

The mind is a conscious collection of thoughts, experiences, emotions, and feelings. It is existential and the vehicle for daily experiential existence. The mind requires no input from the brain and relies solely on our psychological thought processes to function. This is where the ego resides.

The brain cannot "unlearn" how to carry out its physiological duties. Breathing. Blinking. Digestion. Only through a medical or biological event can the brain be crippled and no longer able to function. The brain does not take commands to breathe or blink.

But the mind. Ahhh…the mind. The mind CAN take commands to change its habits and behaviors because the mind is fueled by interpretations of experiences. And we have absolute control over whether we allow the mind to accept those interpretations as positive or negative. We have control over our egos. We can change them. We can nurture them; however, we cannot utilize our IQ to affect such change. We use the resounding power of our emotional intelligence. No machine or medical procedure can make a healthy, mindful ego. Harnessing and utilizing our emotional intelligence is the tool, a tool that we are all equipped with, regardless of what a standardized test told us our IQ was, Just like the mind and the brain are separate, so is IQ and EQ.

Your brain houses your IQ.

Your mind is your EQ.

# Mindfulness versus BrainFULLness

*"Pain of mind is worse than pain of body."*

—Latin Proverb[19]

A mindful ego is ultimately about personal development, building confidence, self-growth, overall health, and wellness. In essence, a mindful ego and emotional intelligence equates to *emotional resilience*. Resilience is the ability to embrace the positive and discern the negative; the ability to identify what is negative and make the personal decision how it will impact you. Search for the positive and allow it to manifest within you for the good of not only yourself, but for others. It is the *lens* through which our mind perceives reality that, in turn, shapes our behaviors and perceptions of reality. It is not the reality itself that shapes us because that is merely a resilient, transient perception. Let mindfulness keep that *lens* free of smudges and dust.

Karramba Production/Shutterstock.com

Karramba Production/Shutterstock.com

Imagine yourself walking across a hillside on a beautiful spring afternoon. It is perfectly warm weather, sun melting upon your skin just enough to balance the crisp breeze that is carrying the amazing scent of iris and lillies and daisies. Every step you take through the bright green carpet of wild grass lifts small scented seedlings that catch the slight breeze and dance effortlessly to their final resting point elsewhere along the hillside. You happen upon a lightly forested area and notice dandelions scattered beneath your feet. Sit down, lift a handful of dandelion seed bundles, and blow gently to release the pods. They float all around you and dance over your shoulders, arms, and gently glide to the ground. Close your eyes, lean back into the sea of white and golden dandelion. Smell the scented air. Feel the warmth upon your skin. Lose yourself in the moment. Not a thought or a care in the world. This moment is yours. All yours.

## BOOM!

The sound of a gunshot in the distance. The lingering echo of something very wrong breaks the hillside silence. You instantly sit up, heart pounding. You feel the deafening thumping in your ears as blood is racing to your head.

What just occurred is an example of mindfulness versus (what I like to call) *brainFULLness*.

Mindfulness was the hillside experience. BrainFULLness was the instantaneous disengagement of the mindful experience and immediate reactionary state that occurred with the gunshot.

The mindful experience lasted 20, 30 minutes on that hillside. You were responding to your experience. The brainFULL experience will last as long as it takes to process the fear of the unknown, and react to your experience, having a physiological "fight or flight" reaction, run down the hill to safety. That brain-FULL experience will be the one thing you talk about amongst friends and social gatherings for the rest of your life. That gunshot in the distance is what you may carry with you whenever you think about that hillside experience. You may not talk about the "moment that was all yours." You will remember and rehash the sound of the gunshot that ended your moment.

To further complicate the matter, every time you see that hillside, or another similar hillside, you may not remember the beauty of the flowers, the scents or the breeze or the dandelions. Your brain will rekindle that terrifying experience.

This is human nature. This is the construct of a lack of mindfulness.

The mind was lost in the moment on that hillside. And the brain was the reactionary response to the unknown; this is where emotional intelligence comes in.

It wasn't a gunshot at all. It was me in my old car on the backside of that hill. The engine is in need of repair and it frequently backfires. It was the backfire of my car that you heard.

Having a mindful ego, and exercising one's emotional intelligence, would have prevented the destruction of the beautiful hillside experience.

By simply acknowledging that there is information out there that is unknown and allowing the ego to assume it had all of that information to draw a conclusion based on the brain's reaction, the healthy mindful experience was lost.

As mentioned earlier in the chapter, it is possible to strengthen our emotional intelligence and develop our mindful egos. It requires practice, however. Allow me to share with you a very simple exercise to jumpstart your mindfulness and set the course for the construct of your new-found ego and emotional intelligence.

First, the stage needs to be set with some background on how effective this technique can be.

One Christmas I brought home a tiny Morkie puppy for my girlfriend. After many months of searching for this particular tiny breed of puppy and doing all of the homework to ensure that the puppy was provided a healthy living environment, two weeks before Christmas I handed Toby over to his new owner. You can imagine how her eyes lit up! I cannot explain to you, without choking up a little, how attached I became to that little guy. He contracted Parvo.

This tiny little puppy was seen by a veterinarian, given medication, was under constant hydration therapy and spent his last week being fed wet food from a syringe. Toby died Christmas morning. In her hands.

I dreaded that next Christmas. My first thought was to avoid the holiday altogether and pretend it didn't exist. Instead, I controlled my emotions and put up a tree, and restrung the holiday lights around the outside of my house. It was Christmas as usual, but every time I walked into my living room, all I saw was that dreadful event that occurred a year ago in that very space. I was overcome with emotion and it overwhelmed me. My brain would NOT let it go! As much as I employed all of the strategies to respond to the virtual emotional "monster" standing in my face, I just could not separate my mind from my brain. For the first time in my mindful adult life, I felt myself crumbling and ill-equipped to respond. I was in full reaction mode. It was clearly the physical proximity to the "monster" that was the problem. So much so that it wouldn't allow the separation between mindfulness and brainFULLness. Something needed to change. I walked upstairs, went outside, and climbed atop my roof. No, don't go there. I wasn't going to do a swan-dive from two stories up.

I sat on my roof and looked around, and what I saw was the absence of anything Christmas. I couldn't see the lights around the edge of my house that greeted me every time I walked toward the front door. I couldn't smell the scent of pine needles as I walked in the house. I couldn't see the tree itself. As I sat on my roof, next to my A/C unit, I was alone. There was no "monster" up there. Instead there were the tops of trees that I had never seen, other rooftops, smoke billowing out of chimneys. There were no visual or sensory reminders for the brain to pick up on.

I changed the mindful venue. I pressed the "reset" button to mindfulness. Because the physical proximity to what was clouding the separation of mind and brain was changed, so was the brain's ability to function resulting in the ability of the mind to start functioning once again, mindfully functioning. Sometimes even the most well-trained level of emotional intelligence needs a change of venue to hit that "reset" button. It is a very simple exercise, and incredibly effective.

Tang Yan Song/Shutterstock.com

## ACTIVITY: DEMONSTRATE YOUR MINDFUL EGO

Describe one of your "hillside experiences":

_____

_____

_____

_____

_____

_____

What was your mindful moment?

_____

_____

_____

_____

_____

_____

How did your brain end that mindful moment?

_____

_____

_____

_____

_____

_____

How could you have utilized your emotional intelligence to preserve that mindful moment?

_____

_____

_____

_____

_____

_____

# Personal Resolution Pyramid[20]

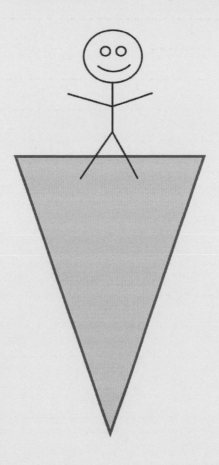

© 2015 Steve W. Peterson

The purpose of the Personal Resolution Pyramid is to simulate balance on three sides of the pyramid so that it rests evenly on the tip. Each of the three sides of the pyramid represents various aspects of one's personal and professional life:

- Past, Present and Future
- Personal, Social and Professional

This is accomplished by mindfully identifying emotional events in each category. The key is to not allow brainFULLness to direct your responses. Exercise a mindful ego and pay attention to your emotional intelligence to guide you. Accept without judgment.

## Pyramid Number One—
## Past, Present, and Future[20]

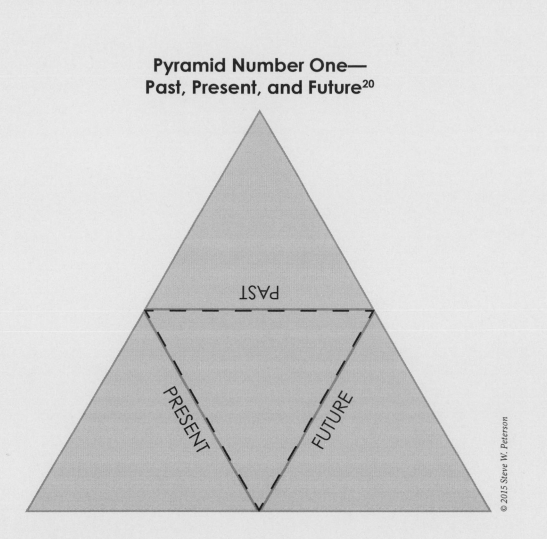

This is a cut-out of your first pyramid.

Once completed, cut along the solid lines and fold along the dotted lines.

Within each category, identify factors significant to your life. Write them in the appropriate categories. You can list as many items as you wish in each category.

The significant factors you need to identify are:

- Goals.
- Stressors.
- Memories.
- Fears.
- Ambitions.
- Concerns.
- Any emotional event that is at the forefront of your mind – positive or negative.

[This Page Intentionally Left Blank]

Now look at how many items you have listed in each category. Odds are, there are an unequal number of items listed.

Your goal is to balance each side of your pyramid. Unless each side has an equal number of items listed, the pyramid will not balance on its tip.

This is where your emotional intelligence gets a workout. Mindfully determine which items can be removed from each category in order to achieve balance. You may need to add items to a category. Determine what is important and what is not. It does not matter whether you have positive or negative events in each category; that is a part of life. The good. And the bad.

It is your emotional intelligence that will guide you on how to respond to these events and come to closure with the negative ones…and relish in the positive ones.

In regards to your goals, be reasonable. We were all told since we were children that we could accomplish ANYTHING that we wanted! There is nothing wrong with childhood and adult aspirations. A mindful ego is reasonable and would rather bask in its successes versus its failures. Be reasonable. A mindful ego uses small successes as the steps to reach the top of the stage where it receives its recognition. Remember it's the journey, not the destination that brings the best reward.

*"If you are depressed you are living in the past.*
*If you are anxious you are living in the future.*
*If you are at peace you are living in the present."*

—Lao Tzu

An online post through social media paraphrased this quite well.

1. The past
   - Everyone has a past; decide wisely what you choose to have influence over you.

2. The future
   - Select reasonable, attainable goals rather than stress over what hasn't happened yet.

3. The present
   - It is how you come to terms with the past and plan for the future that enables you to live in the present!

iQoncept/Shutterstock.com

## Pyramid Number Two—
## Personal, Professional and Social[20]

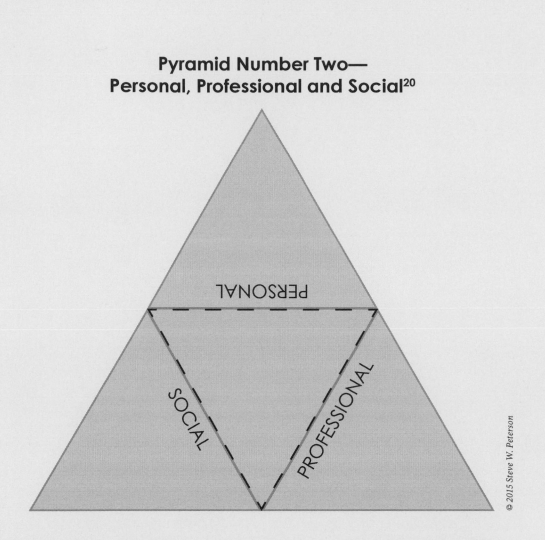

© 2015 Steve W. Peterson

Repeat the same exercise but this time focus on your personal, professional, and social life.

[This Page Intentionally Left Blank]

# References

1. Goleman, D. (2006). *Emotional intelligence*. New York: Bantam Books.

2. *Merriam-Webster.com*. Merriam-Webster, n.d. Accessed 2 Oct. 2014.

3. Whetton, B. 7 Secrets of Emotional Intelligence. *CoreCoaching*. Brian Whetton, 2006. Web. Apr.–May 2014. www.corecoaching.org

4. Moss, E., Cyr, C., & Dubois-Comtois, K. (2004). "Attachment at early school age and developmental risk: examining family contexts and behavior problems of controlling-caregiving, controlling-punitive, and behaviorally disorganized children." *Developmental Psychology*, *40*, 519.

5. Follingstad, D. R., Rutledge, L. L., Berg, B. J., Hause, E. S., & Polek, D. S. (1990). The role of emotional abuse in physically abusive relationships. *Journal of Family Violence*, *5*(2), 107–120.

6. Serby, M., & Yu, M. (2003). Overview: depression in the elderly. *The Mount Sinai Journal of Medicine, New York*, *70*(1), 38–44.

7. *The Qur'an. 2*: 138.

8. Amawattana, T., Mandel, J., & Ekstrand, M. (1994). A pilot study of AIDS education combined with Vipassana meditation among Thai university students. *International Conference on AIDS. 10:344* (abstract no. PD0555).

9. Bruckstein, D. C. (1999). *Effects of acceptance-based and cognitive behavioral interventions on chronic pain management* (Unpublished doctoral dissertation). Hofstra University, USA.

10. Kernis, M. H. (2003). Toward a conceptualization of optimal self-esteem. *Psychological Inquiry*, *14*, 1–26.

11. Mackintosh, N. (2011). P. 169 "after the age of 8–10, IQ scores remain relatively stable: the correlation between IQ scores from age 8 to 18 at age 40 is over 0.70."

12. Salovey, P., & Mayer, J. D. (1989). Emotional intelligence. *Imagination, cognition and personality*, *9*(3), 185–211.

13. Goldstein, A., & Lowery, P. J. (1975, September). " Effect of the opiate antagonist naloxone on body temperature in rats. *Life Sciences 17*(6): 927–31.

14. Schultz, W. (2007). Multiple dopamine functions at different time courses. *Annu. Rev. Neurosci. 30*: 259–88.

15. und Halbach, O. V. B., & Dermietzel, R. (2006). Neurotransmitters and neuromodulators: handbook of receptors and biological effects. *Neurotransmitters and neuromodulators: handbook of receptors and biological effects*. John Wiley & Sons.

16. Boudarene, M., Legros, J. J., Timsit-Berthier, M. (2001). [Study of the stress response: role of anxiety, cortisol and DHEAs]. *L'Encephale*, *28*(2), 139–146.

17. Roosevelt, Franklin D. (April 15, 1939). *Pan American Day address*.

18. Chopra, Deepak. (n.d.). BrainyQuote.com. Retrieved from http://www.brainyquote.com/quotes/quotes/d/deepakchop599977.htm

19. Publilius Syrus quotes (Roman author, 1st century B.C.)

20. Peterson, Steven W. Copyright 2015.

Name _____     Date _____

## CHAPTER 2 QUESTIONS

1. Define ego.

2. By contrast, what is a mindful ego?

3. Compare and contrast IQ (Intelligence Quotient) and EQ (Emotion Quotient).

4. What are the four factors of Salovey and Mayer's model?

5. What are the two chemicals released during period of anxiety and stressful events that put our bodies in a reactive mode (fight or flight/sympathetic mode)?

6. What are the two chemicals released in our bodies during parasympathetic mode?

# MINDFUL AWARENESS REFLECTION JOURNAL

4 Step **MAC** Guide

Choose one mindful experience as you begin your reflection.

### Empathically Acknowledge

Describe your experience.

_____

_____

_____

### Intentional Attention

Describe what you noticed.

| Breath |
|---|
| Body |
| Emotions |
| Thoughts |
| Senses |

### Accept Without Judgment

Describe judgment; acceptance.

_____

_____

_____

### Willingly Choose

Choose to purposely respond to your experience.

_____

_____

_____

### Mindful Mac Meditation

Describe your meditation experiences. What did you learn from your meditation experience?

_____

_____

_____

# Mindful Daily Journal

TODAY'S Insight NOW!

_____

_____

_____

_____

_____

_____

_____

_____

_____

_____

_____

_____

_____

_____

_____

_____

_____

_____

_____

*Tips for Wellbeing*

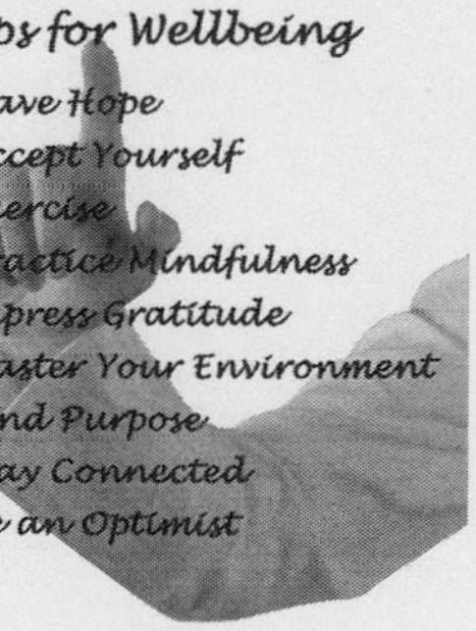

- *Have Hope*
- *Accept Yourself*
- *Exercise*
- *Practice Mindfulness*
- *Express Gratitude*
- *Master Your Environment*
- *Find Purpose*
- *Stay Connected*
- *Be an Optimist*

_____

_____

_____

_____

Date: _____  Make Today Count!

# The Positive Effects of Exercise Across the Lifespan

**Steve Peterson**

*Photo courtesy of Maria Napoli*

*The ocean bathes my senses*

*It challenges my muscles*

*Stretching, moving, flexing*

*We sail together in bliss*

Maria Napoli

*YanLev/Shutterstock.com*

*Karramba Production/Shutterstock.com*

*MJTH/Shutterstock.com*

There is no shortage of public exposure to, or availability of, medical, social-behavioral, and psychological information related to the health and wellness benefits of exercise, nor is it difficult to find a book or televised program exhaustive of information related to diet and exercise. Barnes & Noble[2] offers over 60,000 titles in media and print within the "diet and exercise" category and The Book Depository[3] offers over 15,000 titles under "exercise and workout books." On any particular Sunday morning there are 13 available segments on cable television offering various workout regimens, diet and exercise guidance or products to promote exercise at home.

In 2012, the American Physiological Society published a study that demonstrates that physical inactivity contributes to most of 35 major chronic health conditions, that sedentary behavior increases risks of deteriorating health across the lifespan, that childhood/adolescent activity carries clinical consequences into adulthood, and that physical activity can prevent or delay the onset of chronic diseases.[4]

Yet in that same year, the Centers for Disease Control and Prevention released a report stating that less than 50% of adults met the 2008 Physical Activity Guidelines for aerobic activity and less than 25% met the guidelines for muscle-strengthening activity. Also, only one-third of high school students receive 60 minutes of physical activity every day.[5] This same report identified an alarming behavior of adolescents/adults: nearly 25% reported that they did not participate in ANY physical activity (representative of exercise) in the past month.

# Physical Activity Guidelines for Americans[6]

## Guidelines for Children and Adolescents[6] (Ages 6 to 17)

- Overall recommended: 60 minutes or more of physical activity daily.
- Aerobic: Most of the 60 or more minutes a day should be either moderate or vigorous-intensity aerobic physical activity, and should include vigorous-intensity physical activity at least 3 days a week.

- Muscle-strengthening: As part of the 60 or more minutes of daily physical activity, muscle-strengthening physical activity should be included on at least 3 days of the week.
- Bone-strengthening: As part of the 60 or more minutes of daily physical activity, bone-strengthening physical activity should be included on at least 3 days of the week.

## Guidelines for Adults[6] (Ages 18 to 64)

gpointstudio/Shutterstock.com

- All adults should avoid inactivity. Some physical activity is better than none, and adults who participate in any amount of physical activity gain some health benefits.
- For substantial health benefits, adults should do at least 150 minutes a week of moderate-intensity, or 75 minutes a week of vigorous-intensity aerobic physical activity, or an equivalent combination of moderate- and vigorous-intensity aerobic activity. Aerobic activity should be performed in episodes of at least 10 minutes, and preferably, should be spread throughout the week.
- For additional and more extensive health benefits, adults should increase their aerobic physical activity to 300 minutes a week of moderate intensity, or 150 minutes a week of vigorous intensity aerobic physical activity, or an equivalent combination of moderate- and vigorous-intensity activity. Additional health benefits are gained by engaging in physical activity beyond this amount.
- Adults should also do muscle-strengthening activities that are moderate or high intensity and involve all major muscle groups on 2 or more days a week, as these activities provide additional health benefits.

## Guidelines for Older Adults[6] (Ages 65 and older)

- The Guidelines for Adults also apply to older adults. Additionally, these guidelines apply specifically to older adults:
  - When older adults cannot do 150 minutes of moderate-intensity aerobic activity a week because of chronic conditions, they should be as physically active as their abilities and conditions allow.
  - Older adults should do exercises that maintain or improve balance if they are at risk of falling.
  - Older adults should determine their level of effort for physical activity relative to their level of fitness.
  - Older adults with chronic conditions should understand whether and how their conditions affect their ability to do regular physical activity safely.

auremar/Shutterstock.com

# What Qualifies as Exercise?

*Kapreski/Shutterstock.com*

Many may find the idea of exercise a bit challenging or unattainable either because of an inaccurate definition of what qualifies as exercise or by assuming that exercise must be inclusive of a gym membership and structured activities that have a cost involved.

Exercise is a physical activity that is planned, structured and repetitive for the purpose of conditioning a part of the body, comprised of a series of movements done to become stronger and healthier.[7]

As mentioned previously, it is recommended that individuals in all age groups should participate in some component of active (muscle- and bone-strengthening) exercise as well as aerobic exercise.

Active exercise is motion imparted to a part of the body by voluntary contraction and relaxation of its controlling muscles.[8]

Aerobic exercise is designed to increase oxygen consumption and improve functioning of the cardiovascular and respiratory systems.[8]

To determine if an activity "qualifies" as exercise, anyone of any age can identify a pleasurable exercise/recreational activity that can be *their* exercise as long as it falls within the parameters for active and aerobic activity. These activities can range from the zealous running around and climbing on playground equipment that children participate in, intramural high school activities and hiking with friends for the adolescent, treadmills, or regular yard work for the adult, or working in a garden and walking around the neighborhood for the senior citizen. There are no scripted activity constraints as long as the activity combats a sedentary lifestyle. If someone finds the activity pleasurable and rewarding, they will be more likely to repeat the exercise and commit to a regular regimen.

# Indoor Versus Outdoor Exercises?

*Viktoria Gavrilina/Shutterstock.com*

*Rocksweeper/Shutterstock.com*

There are many variables that affect an individual's indoor versus outdoor exercise choices: personal preference, climate or weather constraints, and the specificity of the activity itself (indoor sport versus individual outdoor activity). Studies suggest that there are mutual benefits to either venue.

Outdoor exercise activities may provide a greater degree of stress relief and energy levels than indoor activities.[9] The connectivity with nature, the exposure to fresh air, and the mental release can provide a more enriching and motivating experience. Some activities just lend themselves to being outdoors. Jogging on a sunny day, water recreation, gardening, etc. have a built-in "nature" component that encourages deeper breathing, mindful awareness of environmental stimuli, and overall distraction from urbanization. Merely being outside for many promotes physical activity. A study of children found that physically activity increased when an activity was held outdoors instead of indoors[10] and older adults tend to exercise for longer period outdoors than indoors.[11]

However, indoor exercise (gym memberships, yoga classes, etc.) tend to promote motivation to work out because of the social setting.[12] An active career and family lifestyle may lend itself to a gym membership or other social indoor activities for the average adult. Many gyms are open 24 hours a day and offer various exercise classes during the lunchtime hours and immediately after work to accommodate the busy adult lifestyle.

Essentially it is the exercise itself that is of greatest importance and benefit, not necessarily the environment within which it is conducted.

## ACTIVITY: IDENTIFY YOUR PHYSICAL ACTIVITY

*"Take care of your body. It's the only place you have to live."*

—Jim Rohn[13]

Answer the following questions by checking/completing the appropriate boxes:

1. On which days did you get at least thirty minutes of exercise last week?

   ☐ Mon   ☐ Tues   ☐ Weds   ☐ Thur   ☐ Fri   ☐ Sat   ☐ Sun

2. How many minutes in each of those days was aerobic exercise?

| Mon | Tues | Weds | Thur | Fri | Sat | Sun |
|-----|------|------|------|-----|-----|-----|
|     |      |      |      |     |     |     |

3. How many minutes in each of those days was a muscle-strengthening exercise?

| Mon | Tues | Weds | Thur | Fri | Sat | Sun |
|-----|------|------|------|-----|-----|-----|
|     |      |      |      |     |     |     |

4. If you need to improve your level of weekly exercise, what are you willing to do?

## Childhood as the Foundational Period of Physical Development and Emotional Well-Being

Physical growth, specifically tissue growth (predominately muscle), occurs at a steady pace between the ages of 2 and 10 in preparation for a final growth spurt during adolescence.[14] Boys grow about 4 inches during their adolescent period and girls approximately 3½ inches.[15]

Proper nutrition and exercise are vital during this period as it is a precursor for final adolescent physical growth and muscular-skeletal development. Exercise reduces body-fat concentration. This is important because studies have shown that elevated levels of saturated fats and adipose tissue prevent muscle enlargement and development; specifically increased levels of inflammation occur (cortisol release), insulin levels are altered, and fibrosis occurs.[16] These events contribute to atrophy and inhibited muscle development. A Centers for Disease Control and Prevention report in 2014 identified that in the United States 8.4% of 2- to 5-year olds were considered obese, as well as 17.7% of 6- to 11-year olds.[17] Obesity is defined as having excess body fat, a result of caloric imbalance from too few calories expended compared to the amount of calories consumed.[18]

Weight control, improved strength and endurance, improved cholesterol and blood pressure levels as well as improved muscle and bone growth are all clinical results of regular childhood physical activity.[19] Also, it is suggested that this regular physical activity can reduce the risks of childhood diabetes and later onset of cardiovascular disease.

In addition to physiological benefits, it has been demonstrated that schoolchildren who are physically active tend to perform better academically.[20] This can be related to improved cognitive ability and stability, but also a healthy level of self-esteem.

The health and wellness of a child's self-esteem can be contributed to many factors. However, taking into consideration the degree that a child's social development is impacted by school and its related childhood interactions, it is important to lend credence to the impact that exposure has to a child's self-esteem and self-image. School-age bullying has gained national attention as a very real and destructive presence in our school systems, leading to reports of clinical depression and, unfortunately, suicides. Nearly 28% of students report having been bullied during the school year.[21] Of those, nearly half were harassed because of their looks and one-third because of their body shape.[22]

What used to be commonly accepted (an arguably a poor social norm) as a "rite of passage" and test of a child's visceral ability to handle confrontation has become exacerbated by the introduction and proliferation of social media. Cyberbullying has intensified physical bullying and created a very concerning problem and new reality for today's youth.

Whether low self-image and self-esteem contributes to one becoming bullied or is a result of being bullied is debatable. Regardless, at stake is a child's self-esteem. However, if low self-esteem may put a child at greater risk of being a victim, then there is evidence to support that regular exercise can contribute to a child's sense of self-worth and self-esteem by combating obesity and improving body self-image.[23] As a correlation, improved self-image may also help a child deal with the effects of bullying and other negative extrinsic influences.[24]

## Adolescence Is a World of Change

The adolescent years can effectively be characterized as a period wrought with social pressures and stigma, strong hormonal release, emotional highs and lows, enhanced perception of personal image and the need to create a sense of self-identity. There are a lot of stressful events facing the average adolescent, and mechanisms to assist with these stresses are very much needed. Of all intrinsic and extrinsic stressors, exercise can be a formidable tool in addition to mindfulness.

Antonio Guillem/Shutterstock.com

Body image is of great importance to adolescents of either gender. Exercise not only plays a role in maintenance of body fat composition and muscle development/toning, but also in the maintenance, health and development of the largest organ in the human body—the skin, with an average adult surface area of 18 square feet.[25] Exercise increases circulation, improves blood flow, causes perspiration, and boosts oxygenation, all of which help replenish nutrients to the skin and prevent dryness. Additionally, collagen production is increased which helps plump and maintain flexibility in the skin.[26]

Pressmaster/Shutterstock.com

Healthy coping with emotional highs and lows and transient depression during adolescence (especially in females) can have an impact on ability to effectively respond to similar stressors in early adulthood.[27] Exercise elicits the release of endorphins, which has a positive correlation to an overall improved mood and psychological well-being.[28] Endorphins impose an analgesic effect upon the body, and increases in physical activity promote continued endorphin release. Exercise and physical activity can have a similarly beneficial impact on symptoms of depression as do some antidepressant treatments.[29,30]

The social network for an adolescent helps promote a sense of identity and belonging; therefore it stands to reason that participation in group sports activities leads to increased levels of self-esteem and social connectivity. Even non-organized, small groups of friends participating in social physical activities can have this same outcome. Involvement in exercise with friends can also serve as a sense of motivation for an otherwise "unmotivated" teen.

Exercise can also improve the immune system response, specifically in those prone to maladaptive stress responses.[31] Many adolescents, due to combined physiological and psychological forces mentioned earlier, put themselves in a compromised immune status due to proliferation of the sympathetic nervous system response. Lack of a mindful and healthy response to intrinsic and extrinsic stressors elicits this sympathetic response, which studies have shown compromise the immune system.[31]

## ACTIVITY: CHILDHOOD EXERCISE AND ADOLESCENT BENEFITS

*"The developmental decline and benefits of exercise are documented; however, relatively little is known about the mechanisms and motivations underlying adolescent exercise behavior."* [32]

Identify some childhood exercise activities that can become exercise habits for adolescents

| Childhood | | Adolescent |
|---|---|---|
| *Example:*<br>*Little League Sport* | ⟶ | *High School*<br>*Sport/Intramurals* |
| *Example:*<br>*Jogging With Parents* | ⟶ | *Recreational*<br>*Outdoor Running* |
| | ⟶ | |
| | ⟶ | |
| | ⟶ | |
| | ⟶ | |
| | ⟶ | |

In your opinion, what is the primary reason that inactive adolescents do not exercise?



How could that behavior be changed?

## Adulthood: Time to Renew or Implement Good Exercise Habits

Generally speaking, adulthood can be the busiest and most complicated period of our lives. Responsibilities are now aplenty, decisions now rest solely on our shoulders, financial burdens are newly acquired, and starting a family is either being considered or has already started, and navigation through a career has begun. In general, the adult terrain can be quite fast-paced and relatively unforgiving. As adults we are constantly being drawn in a dozen directions at once and our attention being pulled away from ourselves and required of others.

*Monkey Business Images/Shutterstock.com*

Being mindful of one's personal exercise needs, let alone finding time for exercise, can easily slide down the ladder of priorities. Ironically, this is the period of our lives where being mindful of, and attending to, our own personal, physical and mental needs will equip us to better handle the challenges lying ahead of us. This is crucial if we want to have a healthy and fruitful life when we are much older.

Chronic diseases and conditions are the leading causes of death and disability, according to the Centers for Disease Control and Prevention. The most commonly identified non-communicable diseases in the United States that account for nearly 7 of the top 10 causes of death are heart disease, diabetes, stroke, cancer and obesity.[33] In 2010 48% of adult deaths were caused by cancer and heart disease.[33] In 2012 it was reported that half of all American adults have one or more chronic health conditions.[34] The CDC further notes that, including arthritis, these are among the most common and preventable of health problems.

*Photo courtesy of Maria Napoli*

Overall, there is strong evidence that active adult men and women not only have lower rates of chronic disease states and conditions, they are better able to maintain a stable and healthy weight maintenance and as they become older are less likely to suffer hip or vertebral fracture.[35]

For those looking to start a family, it has been shown that obesity contributes to increased risk of female infertility[36] and that moderate exercise can help maintain male sexual libido.[37]

In addition to *making* time for exercise, it is important to recognize that opportunities for exercise are abundant and readily available in most people's everyday lives. If one were to categorize opportunities for adults to engage in physical activity, it may look something like this:

- Leisure time (swimming, hiking, gardening, walking, dancing)
- Occupational (blue-collar laborer, construction)
- Household chores
- Sports
- Planned exercise
- Family activities/Outings
- Community activities/Social involvement
- Commuting (walking, cycling)

Exercise may be an everyday occurrence for many, but the key is to maintain a consistency and regularity in activity to maximize benefits and allow exercise to become a routine. For some a change of venue may help contribute to establishing an exercise routine. Going to a gym, going outside, or finding a separate and unique location for one's exercise can provide a "personal" space and means of escape.

Becoming involved in group physical activities can be of benefit because it offers the social component that can serve as not only a motivator but also a distraction from the day's burdens.

## Older Adults: Relish and Maintain

CREATISTA/Shutterstock.com

Older adults stand to benefit from the health and wellness practices instituted when they were younger. Lifelong exercise habits exert influence on the perceived benefits and willingness to participate as we become older; however, at this point in life, it would behoove one to continue to look forward and make sure the body is a "temple" and not an "empty playground." Physical activity may be a bit less exciting and become bound by age-related constraints, but it does not hold any less value or short- and long-term gains.

Particularly in elderly populations, exercise has been shown to protect the brain from neurodegeneration by increasing synaptic plasticity and also by assisting with learning and memory.[38]

Loss of muscle mass and strength related to age contributes to increased disability (if applicable), frailty, and falls. Regular exercise for this age group can reduce the risk of osteoporosis and other age-related debilitating conditions, as well as improving sleep and reducing depression.[39]

Social support, accessibility, and safety[40] all play key roles in promoting exercise activities for this particular age group. Perceived barriers to exercise need also be broken down, as there are many types of physical activity one can safely participate in.

| Aerobic Activities for Older Adults | Muscle-Strengthening Activities for Older Adults |
|---|---|
| • Walking<br>• Dancing<br>• Swimming<br>• Water aerobics<br>• Jogging<br>• Aerobic exercise classes<br>• Bicycle riding (stationary or on a path)<br>• Some activities of gardening, such as raking and pushing a lawn mower<br>• Tennis<br>• Golf (without a cart) | • Exercises using exercise bands, weight machines, hand-held weights<br>• Callisthenic exercises (body weight provides resistance to movement)<br>• Digging, lifting, and carrying as part of gardening<br>• Carrying groceries<br>• Some yoga exercises<br>• Some Tai chi exercises |

# Nutrition and Exercise: Protein and Hydration

Ensuring the body receives its proper nutritional requirements during the course of exercise is, obviously, very important. Portion control, introduction of fruits and vegetables, and monitoring carbohydrate and fat intake are all crucial components. Exercise increases the body's nutritional demand substantially more than that of a sedentary lifestyle. Having a well-balanced, healthy diet with proper hydration will help 1) facilitate an effective exercise regimen, 2) reduce injuries, and 3) promote recovery. When these three components are addressed it is much easier to maintain an exercise routine and find enjoyment in it.[41]

FikMik/Shutterstock.com

Protein is not only important for muscle growth and tissue repair, but can also be a source of energy for those who are monitoring their carbohydrate intake. Protein slows the release of carbohydrates into the bloodstream and can prevent sudden spikes in blood sugar that can encourage fat storage and unstable energy levels, [42] as well as prevent skeletal muscle loss. For the mature and older adult, dietary protein needs increase with muscle-strengthening exercise.[43]

It is widely held that the average American consumes twice as much as protein as is required.[44] This is of concern because a sedentary lifestyle will not sufficiently utilize the protein and too much protein in the diet can increase dehydration and will be stored in the body as fat; consequently, many are not aware of some of the healthier sources of protein and where the greatest concentration of protein exists; this is important because of portion-control in the diet. Leaner, healthier sources of protein can be ingested in smaller portions than an unhealthier counterpart with a greater fat content.

## Healthy Sources of Protein[42]

It is important to be mindful of MSG, sodium, nitrates, and preservatives in any food item when trying to achieve maximum nutritional value.

alexpro9500/Shutterstock.com

nevodka/Shutterstock.com

lsantilli/Shutterstock.com

_Dairy_

Greek Yogurt—18 g per 8 oz

Cottage Cheese—14 g per ½ cup

Swiss Cheese—8 g per 1 oz

Eggs—6 g per 1 large egg

2% Milk—8 g per 1 cup

Soy Milk—8 g per 1 cup

_Meat_

Steak (lean cut)—23 g per 3 oz

Ground Beef (90% lean)—18 g per 3 oz

Pork Chops (boneless)—26 g per 3 oz

Chicken Breast (boneless, skinless)—24 g per 3 oz

Turkey Breast—24 g per 3 oz

*Alexander/Shutterstock.com*

*grynold/Shutterstock.com*

### Seafood

Yellowfin Tuna—25 g per 3 oz

Halibut—23 g per 3 oz

Octopus—25 g per 3 oz

Sockeye Salmon—23 g per 3 oz

Tilapia—21 g per 3 oz

### Canned Foods

Anchovies—24 g per 3 oz

Light Tuna—22 g per 3 oz

Chicken—21 g per 3 oz

Sardines—21g per 3 oz

Navy Beans—20 g per 1 cup

Dried Lentils—13 g per ¼ cup

*Berents/Shutterstock.com*

*Madlen/Shutterstock.com*

### Deli Meats

Roast Beef—18 g per 3 oz

Roasted Turkey Breast—18 g per 3 oz

### Grains

Wheat Germ—6 g per ½ cup

Soba Noodles—12 g per 3 oz

Quinoa—8 g per 1 cup

# Proper Hydration

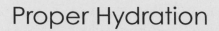

*Africa Studio/Shutterstock.com*

The body's fluid intake, especially during periods of exercise, is essential because water helps regulate body temperature through sweating, it facilitates digestion and lubrication of joints and body tissues.

Exercise can lead to substantial water and electrolyte loss and sufficient replenishment can help maintain exercise performance. Improper replenishment can lead to dehydration with such signs as muscle fatigue, decreased energy, loss of coordination and heat illness.[45] The American College of Sports Medicine suggests the following guidelines:

| Hydration Before Exercise | Hydration During Exercise | Hydration After Exercise |
|---|---|---|
| 16–20 oz 4 hours before<br><br>8–12 oz 15 minutes before | 3–8 oz every 15–20 minutes | Correct fluid losses within two hours—amount varies on amount of sweat |

# References

1. Hippocrates. (n.d.). BrainyQuote.com. Retrieved February 14, 2015 from http://www.brainyquote.com/quotes/quotes/h/hippocrate153531.html

2. http://www.barnesandnoble.com/ This was a Web site search to determine that this company offers over 60,000 titles in media and print within the "diet and exercise" category.

3. http://www.bookdepository.com/ This was a Web site search to determine that this company offers over 15,000 titles under "exercise and workout books".

4. Booth, F. W., Roberts, C. K., & Laye, M. J. (2012). Lack of exercise is a major cause of chronic diseases. *Comprehensive Physiology.*

5. Centers for Disease Control and Prevention: Division of Nutrition, Physical Activity, and Obesity. (DATE). http://www.cdc.gov/nccdphp/dnpao/index.html

6. Office of Disease Prevention and Health Promotion. (2008). *2008 physical activity guidelines for American's summary.* Accessed 12 Feb 2015. http://health.gov/paguidelines/guidelines/summary.as

7. Exercise. (n.d.) *Farlex Partner Medical Dictionary.* (2012).

8. Exercise. (n.d.) *Dorland's Medical Dictionary for Health Consumers.* (2007).

9. Thompson, C. J., Boddy, K., Stein, K., Whear, R., Barton, J., et al. (2011). Does participating in physical activity in outdoor natural environments have a greater effect on physical and mental wellbeing than physical activity indoors? PenCLAHRC, Peninsula College of Medicine and Dentistry, University of Exeter, United Kingdom. *Environmental Science Technology, 2011 Mar 1:45*(5):1761–72.

10. Pearce, M., Page, A. S., Griffin, T. P., & Cooper, A. R. (2014). Who children spend time with after school: Associations with objectively recorded indoor and outdoor physical activity. *International Journal of Behavioral Nutrition and Physical Activity, 11*(1), 45.

11. Kerr, J., Sallis, J. F., Saelens, B. E., Cain, K., Conway, T. L., Frank, L. D., & King, A. C. (2012). Outdoor physical activity and self rated health in older adults living in two regions of the US. *Int J Behav Nutr Phys Act, 9*(4).

12. Unger, J. B., Johnson C. A. Department of Preventive Medicine, University of Southern California, Los Angeles, USA. (1995). Social relationships and physical activity in health club members. *American Journal of Health Promotion, 1995 May–Jun;9*(5):340–3.

13. Costanza, S. (2012). *Subject Guides.* Health Education. Montante Family Library Subject Guide. http://dyc.libguides.com/healtheducation

14. Stettler, N., Bhatia, J., Parish. A., & Stallings, V. A. Feeding healthy infants, children, and adolescents. (2011). In: Kliegman, R. M., Behrman, R. E., Jenson, H. B., Stanton, B. F., eds. *Nelson Textbook of Pediatrics*, 19th ed., chapter 42. Philadelphia, PA: Saunders Elsevier.

15. Physical growth of infants and children. *Growth and Development: Merck Manual Professional.* http://www.merckmanuals.com/professional/pediatrics/growth-and-development/physical-growth-of-infants-and-children.

16. Spencer, M., Aiwei Yao-Borengasser, Unal, R., Rasouli, N., Gurley, C. M., Zhu, B., Peterson, C. A., & Kern, P. A. (2010, December). Adipose tissue macrophages in insulin-resistant subjects are associated with collagen VI and fibrosis and demonstrate alternative activation. *American Journal of Physiology—Endocrinology and Metabolism.* December 2010 Vol. 299 no. 6, E1016–E1027 DOI: 10.1152/ajpendo.00329

17. Ogden, C. L., Carroll, M. D., Kit, B. K., & Flegal, K. M. (2014). Prevalence of childhood and adult obesity in the United States, 2011–2012. *Jama, 311*(8), 806-814.

18. Krebs, N. F., Himes, J. H., Jacobseon, D., Nicklas, T. A., Guilday, P., & Styne, D. (2007). Assessment of child and adolescent overweight and obesity. *Pediatrics 2007* 120:S193–S228.

19. U.S. Department of Health and Human Services. (2008). *Physical activity guidelines advisory committee report.* Washington, DC; U.S. Department of Health and Human Services, 2008.

20. Singh, A., Uijtdewilligen, L., Twisk, J. W., Van Mechelen, W., & Chinapaw, M. J. (2012). Physical activity and performance at school: a systematic review of the literature including a methodological quality assessment. *Archives of pediatrics & adolescent medicine, 166*(1), 49–55. doi:10.1001

21. U.S. Department of Education, National Center for Educational Statistics (2013). *Student reports of bullying and cyberbullying: Results from the 2011 school crime supplement to the national crime victimization survey. https://nces.ed.gov/*

22. Davis, S., & Nixon, C. (2010). The youth voice research project: Victimization and strategies. http://njbullying.org/documents/YVPMarch2010.pdf

23. Pierce, J. W., & Wardle, J. (1997), Cause and effect beliefs and self-esteem of overweight children. *Journal of Child Psychology and Psychiatry, 38*: 645–650. doi: 10.1111/j.1469-7610.1997.tb01691.x

24. Strauss, R. S. (2000). Childhood obesity and self-esteem. *Pediatrics, 105*(1), e15-e15.

25. Thompson, R. A., & Calkins, S. D. (1996). The double-edged sword: Emotional regulation for children at risk. *Development and Psychopathology,8*(01), 163–182.

26. Avery, N. C., & Bailey, A. J. (2005). Enzymic and non-enzymic cross-linking mechanisms in relation to turnover of collagen: Relevance to aging and exercise. *Scandinavian Journal of Medicine & Science in Sports, 15*(4), 231–240.

27. Thapar, A., Collishaw, S., Pine, D. S., & Thapar, A. K. (2012). Depression in adolescence. *The Lancet, 379*(9820), 1056–1067.

28. Harber, V. J., & Sutton, J. R. (1984). Endorphins and exercise. *Sports Medicine, 1*(2), 154–171.

29. Pierce, E. F., Eastman, M. W., Tripathi, H. L., Olson, K. G., & Dewey, W. L. (1993). ß-Endorphin response to endurance exercise: relationship to exercise dependence. *Perceptual and motor skills, 77*(3), 767–770.

30. Dinas, P. C., Koutedakis, Y., & Flouris, A. D. (2011). Effects of exercise and physical activity on depression. *Irish Journal of Medical Science, 180*(2), 319–325.

31. Hoffman-Goetz, L., & Pedersen, B. K. (1994). Exercise and the immune system: a model of the stress response? *Immunology Today, 15*(8), 382–387.

32. Nigg, C. R. (2001). Explaining adolescent exercise behavior change: A longitudinal application of the transtheoretical model. *Annals of Behavioral Medicine, 23*(1), 11–20.

33. Centers for Disease Control and Prevention. Death and Mortality. NCHS FastStats Web site. http://www.cdc.gov/nchs/fastats/deaths.htm. Accessed December 20, 2013.

34. Ward, B. W., Schiller, J. S., & Goodman, R. A. (2012). Multiple chronic conditions among US adults: A 2012 update. *Prev Chronic Dis.* 2014;11:130389. DOI: http://dx.doi.org/10.5888/pcd11.130389

35. World Health Organization. Global recommendations on physical activity for health—adults. Retrieved from http://www.who.int/dietphysicalactivity/pa/en/index.html.

36. Wilkes, S., & Murdoch, A. (2009). Obesity and female fertility: A primary care perspective. *Journal of Family Planning and Reproductive Health Care, 35*(3), 181–185.

37. Cormie, P., Newton, R. U., Taaffe, D. R., Spry, N., Joseph, D., Hamid, M. A., & Galvao, D. A. (2013). Exercise maintains sexual activity in men undergoing androgen suppression for prostate cancer: a randomized controlled trial. *Prostate Cancer and Prostatic Diseases, 16*(2), 170–175

38. Cotman, C. W., Berchtold, N. C., & Christie, L. A. (2007). Exercise builds brain health: key roles of growth factor cascades and inflammation. *Trends in neurosciences, 30*(9), 464–472.

39. Seguin, R., & Nelson, M. E. (2003). The benefits of strength training for older adults. *American Journal of Preventive Medicine, 25*(3), 141–149.

40. Rodiek, S. *Access to Nature: Planning Outdoor Space for Aging.* College Station, TX: Center for Health Systems & Design, Texas A&M University

41. Office of Disease Prevention and Health Promotion. (2015). Active older adults. *2008 Physical Activity Guidelines for Americans: Chapter 5*. Accessed 2 Feb. 2015. http://health.gov

42. Kadey, Matthew, MS, RD. (2014). The ultimate list of 40 high-protein foods! http://www.bodybuilding.com/fun/ultimate-list-40-high-protein-foods.html N.p., 17 Sept. 2014. Web. 3 Feb 2015.

43. Evans, W. J. Protein nutrition, exercise, and aging. (2004). *Journal of the American College of Nutrition, 23*(sup6), 601S–609S.

44. U.S. National Library of Medicine. Nutrition and athletic performance: MedlinePlus medical encyclopedia. *U.S. National Library of Medicine*. Accessed 15 Jan 2015. https://www.nlm.nih.gov/medlineplus/

45. Bushman, B. A. (2013). Exercise in the Heat and Adequate Hydration. *ACSM's Health & Fitness Journal, 17*(4), 4–7.

Name _____  Date _____

## CHAPTER 3 QUESTIONS

1.  What is the definition of exercise?

2.  What is the difference between active and aerobic exercise?

3.  What are the potential benefits of outdoor versus indoor activities?

4.  What are some benefits of childhood exercise?

5. What are some contributing factors to adult inactivity?

6. What are some low-impact exercises that older adults can participate in?

7. What three things will having a well-balanced, healthy diet with proper hydration do?

# MINDFUL AWARENESS REFLECTION JOURNAL

4 Step MAC Guide

Mindfully
acknowledge
attention
accept
choose

Choose one mindful experience as you begin your reflection.

## Empathically Acknowledge

Describe your experience.

_____

_____

_____

## Intentional Attention

Describe what you noticed.

| |
|---|
| Breath |
| Body |
| Emotions |
| Thoughts |
| Senses |

## Accept Without Judgment

Describe judgment; acceptance.

_____

_____

_____

## Willingly Choose

Choose to purposely respond to your experience.

_____

_____

_____

## Mindful Mac Meditation

Describe your meditation experiences. What did you learn from your meditation experience?

_____

_____

_____

# Mindful Daily Journal

TODAY'S insight NOW!

_____

_____

_____

_____

_____

_____

_____

_____

_____

_____

_____

_____

_____

_____

_____

_____

_____

_____

*Tips for Wellbeing*

- Have Hope
- Accept Yourself
- Exercise
- Practice Mindfulness
- Express Gratitude
- Master Your Environment
- Find Purpose
- Stay Connected
- Be an Optimist

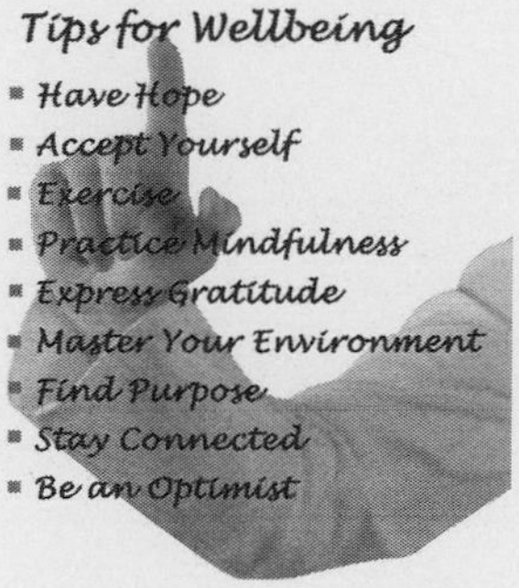

_____

_____

_____

_____

Date: _____  Make Today Count!

# CHAPTER 4

# The Healing Power of Play, Laughter, and Humor

**Steve Peterson**

*I laugh*

*I smile*

*I play*

*Life is good*

Maria Napoli

Play, laughter, and humor are generally synonymous with positive emotions and the production of a smile! It is said that a smile is contagious. The moment someone walks into a room with a beaming smile across their face, the energy of that smile often transfers onto the faces of others. A smile is a universal non-verbal cue; the message of acceptance, being pleased, appearing kind or becoming amused[1] spans across languages, ethnic groups, and cultures. The simple act of smiling releases endorphins, serotonin and dopamine, which help relax the body and reduce blood pressure, decrease anxious feelings, and lower the heart rate.[2]

The release of dopamine, as it is associated with the brain's system of reward recognition, has been correlated with activation of areas of the brain that increase ability to learn and improve one's attention span.[3] Dopamine release can even be triggered vicariously through someone else's smile.[4,5]

Melissa King/Shutterstock.com

Some *fast facts* about the power of a smile:

- Smiling makes us appear more attractive to others, promotes our attraction to others, and lifts the mood of those around us.[6]

- Serotonin release from the act of smiling acts as an anti-depressant.[7]

- A "Duchenne smile" is characterized by curling the muscles along the side of the mouth to such a degree as to show teeth as well as contraction of the muscles along the sides of the eyes.[8] A "less-than-genuine" smile is void of much tooth exposure and eye contraction.

- Even a "less-than-genuine" smile can have similar effects on one-self and others as a true Duchenne smile.[9,10]

Doglikehorse/Shutterstock.com

## ACTIVITY: WHAT MAKES YOU SMILE?

*"In her smile I am reminded that it is the simple things in life that matter. For just a moment, my hurried existence is slowed enough to recognize that the human spirit is much stronger than the body."*

- Kristene Diggins, MSN, RN[11]

Before beginning this activity, spend a little time being mindful of strangers around you, your physical surroundings, and those you interact with. Allow your level of awareness to be heightened and immerse yourself in the moment of an experience. Without allowing judgment, become hypersensitive to what elicits a positive emotion and allow that positive emotion to make an impact on you.

1.  Identify an experience that left you feeling happy and that put a big, genuine smile on your face:

    _____

    _____

    _____

2.  Now articulate your emotions during that experience. How did it make you feel, specifically?

    _____

    _____

    _____

3.  Were you distracted, anxious, or generally inattentive prior to that experience?

    ☐ Yes    ☐ No

    If you answered, "Yes," then explain how long that positive feeling you gained from the experience stayed with you before you returned to your previous thoughts:

    _____

    _____

    _____

## Only Children Play?

If play could be described as perhaps any sort of activity that is for pure enjoyment and recreation without any formal, practical, or serious purpose…then at what point did this word acquire such a negative connotation for adolescents and adults? As one becomes older, the term "play" often becomes associated with lack of responsibility, failure to stay on task, and childish behavior. This is very unfortunate, because for a child playtime leads to happiness, smiling, humor, and laughter.

Hibrida/Shutterstock.com

Humor and the resulting laughter, regardless of one's age, not only provides a personal sensation of feeling uplifted and has a stress-relieving effect on the body[12], but also increases respiratory depth and improves oxygen consumption. Following a good belly laugh, the body experiences a period of muscle relaxation and decrease in respiratory and heart rate.[13] These are mental and physiological benefits that can contribute to the health and well-being of anyone at any age and throughout the entire lifespan! Along the lines of healthcare palliative treatment, Dr. Morse wrote that "since there are no negative side effects (to humor and laughter), they should be used…to reduce stress and pain and to improve healing." [14]

It therefore stands to reason that play be accepted back into the lexicon for adolescents and adults of all ages; not as a regressive or immature behavior, but one of efficacy and with a health/wellness benefit.

## Children and the Implications of a Playful Nature

*"Decades of research have documented that play has a crucial role in the optimal growth, learning and development of children from infancy through adolescence…The time has come to advocate strongly in support of play for all children."*

—Isenberg & Quisenberry[15]

*Dasha Petrenko/Shutterstock.com*

Humor is more readily facilitated when one is in a playful mood. This includes both demonstrating a humorous interaction and being receptive to another's humor. Playfulness can be considered a "prerequisite" to humor." [16] For a child, play and the ensuing aspect of fun are important not only to healthy brain development,[17] but they also afford children the opportunity to explore and conquer their fears, build personal confidence, and better equip them to handle life's upcoming challenges.[18-20]

A fun environment not only facilitates a child's ability to learn,[21] but also strengthens social relationships and helps children find a social construct within which to fit.[22,23] Essentially, playful interaction provides children with a sense of belonging.

Parents may want to ensure their children have an activity-rich and extracurricular experience growing up, but the degree to which children are allowed free play and their own creative time can have an impact on their ability to navigate the pressures and stress they experience growing up, as well as provide a healthy foundation for responding to stress later in life.[24,25]

The application of playfulness, humor, and laughter as an anxiety-reduction tool has become embraced by the pediatric health and dental care communities. Many children's hospitals, pediatric wards, and pedodontic offices have incorporated fun themes, colorful and whimsical designs, and playful animal characters to provide a welcoming and relaxed patient environment.

For many children, medical and dental experiences are cause for great anxiety and the assumption of pain and discomfort. A child's pre-determined thoughts of the situation, even if the situation/procedure is not harmful, can intensify their aversion to it.[26]

mikeledray/Shutterstock.com

More and more research indicates that the introduction of playful, colorful, and inviting environments for pediatric patients is not only conducive to well-being and recovery,[27] but also that humor and laughter are acceptable practices to reduce fear and anxiety in the hospital setting.[28]

In pediatric dental offices, creating a playful, humorous, and fun atmosphere not only reduces initial anxiety, but also helps with systematic desensitization. It is suggested that humor in the pedodontic setting also serves emotional, informational, and motivational functions.[29]

## Adolescents Need Play, Too!

*"The opposite of play is not work; it is depression."*

—Brian Sutton-Smith[30]

At this point it is necessary to distinguish recreation for entertainment from playfulness which results in smiles, laughter, and perhaps humor. The purpose for this clarification is that according to a Nielsen survey, U.S. adolescents age 13 and older spend an average of 6.3 hours a week playing video and computer games[31] as a source of recreation. A 2013 survey by this same company revealed that of 112 hours per month of mixed media as entertainment, the average adolescent dedicated 99 of those hours to television viewing.[32] Unfortunately, it cannot be determined what genre of entertainment the bulk of this media actually is. If it were comedy, sporting events and the like, then it could be safely assumed that this form of entertainment would be playful and provide the benefits of laughter and humor. If that is not the case, then it is important to ensure that there are some playful outlets available to the adolescent.

YanLev/Shutterstock.com

Adolescents employ various coping strategies to deal with their stress and anxiety. Plancherel and Bolognini identified gender differences in these strategies, but also an underlying similarity. Females tend to invest in social relationship as a coping mechanism, whereas males may practice sports or use a sense of humor.[33] As mentioned previously, building a healthy social network requires an emotionally-positive foundation often rooted in commonalities and some component of fun.[22, 23] Having a sense of humor and laughing is stress-relieving to the body[12] as is participating in group activities.[34]

gwolters/Shutterstock.com

Ross Petukhov/Shutterstock.com

Rido/Shutterstock.com

Common to both females and males in this age group is the impact stress has upon their immune systems. Distress increases such stress hormones as beta-endorphins (chemicals produced that act as a pain-suppressant; elevated levels indicative of pain, hypertension, and stress)[35], catecholamines (increase cardiac output, blood vessel constriction, elevate blood pressure, and increase the level of lipids in the blood)[36] and corticotropins (stimulate the sympathetic nervous system, releasing epinephrine and norepinephrine)[37], which suppress the body's natural killer (NK) cells[38] and contribute to immune-suppression. However, it was found that laughter decreased these particular stress hormones and fortified the activity of the natural killer (NK) cells, effectively keeping the immune system strong.[39]

Establishing romantic relationships is one of many identifying behaviors and rites of passage of the adolescent years. Literature and research review indicates a common trait held desirable by both males and females in dating preferences and mate selection is a sense of humor! Males engaged in humor as a courtship ritual and emphasized the importance of their partners' receptivity; females tend to value their partners' ability to produce humor.[40] Utilizing humor as part of relationship conflict resolution was also found to be one of the most effective and desirable techniques and contributed to healthier and longer-lasting relationships.[41] Having a healthy dose of humor and laughter in a relationship has been contributed to not only overall relationship satisfaction, but also perceived ability to cope with other stressors in life.[42]

The adolescent years also indicate the successful completion of high school education and, for some, further education/training of some post-secondary fashion. Either way, success in the classroom is of paramount importance, be it for immediate graduation or establishing effective and successful study habits for a future educational commitment.

Humor has been shown to build social relationships; let it not be forgotten that there is a relationship connection built between a teacher and the student. Maintaining a level of reciprocity in humor and fun in the classroom helps build that connection, whereby enhancing the learning process and helping reduce anxiety about some of the more difficult subjects for the student. Humor not only acts as a stress-reliever for students, but also helps them learn more effectively and provides a greater level of academic satisfaction.[43] Maintaining a modicum degree of levity and allowing adolescents to engage in humor or fun activities can help provide a feeling of psychological safety and afford them a greater opportunity to absorb the material.[44]

## ACTIVITY: LAUGHTER AS A DISTRACTION

*"Laughter is an instant vacation."*

—Milton Berle[45]

Whenever possible, stop whatever it is you are doing and engage in some sort of comedy/humorous event. This can be as simple as watching YouTube™, finding some funny quote on any social media site, or watching a comedian or funny program on Netflix™. Something…anything…that makes you laugh.

1. Now that you are done with your comedy/humor distraction…do you remember what was on your mind beforehand?

_____

_____

_____

2. If you watched a comedy, did you find that you lost track of time?

_____

_____

_____

3. If you watched something on YouTube™ or looked at something on a social media site or the Internet, did you find yourself searching for additional/related items?

_____

_____

_____

4. Did you find that your "comedy relief" actually distracted you from your previous thoughts?

_____

_____

_____

# Stop Acting Like an Adult All the Time

Adults need to find time to play because it helps them forget about commitments, responsibilities, and career for a brief period. It may be a challenge for many adults to engage in a fun and playful activity without accomplishing a goal. There need not be any specific purpose other than to enjoy oneself and socialize in a creative, unstructured, and whimsical way.

The same physiological and psychological benefits of childhood and adolescent play, laughter, and humor apply to adults. In some contexts ten minutes of hearty belly laughing can have the same benefit of two hours of relaxed sleep.[46] Unfortunately, the willingness to participate in and commit to maintain-

ing a healthy level of playfulness and laughter appears to wane as one becomes older and more entrenched in their careers. It is important to talk about the benefits of playfulness, humor, and laughter and the effect it can have on time spent in the workplace.

A 2013–2014 Gallup survey reports that the average American spends 47–50 hours per week at their place of employment.[47] Being happy during work hours would equate to being happy during the majority of their week. A happy employee takes better care of themselves both physically and emotionally[48], fosters and maintains healthy relationships with coworkers, enjoys their work more and is more productive.[49] Happiness and laughter in the workplace boosts morale, promotes creative ideas, and fosters a sense of camaraderie among workers.[46]

In January 2015 nearly 3%, or 3.5 million full-time employees, missed at least two days of work due to personal illness or a medically-related appointment.[50] Although it is not known to what degree this absenteeism was specifically stress related, it is very clear that stress contributes to many medical illnesses and disease states.[51] Earlier studies have indicated that those workers who experienced high levels of stress were twice as likely to be absent a week or longer during the course of a year.[52]

Whether an individual has the opportunity for a bit of playtime, laughter, or humor at work or brings a playful disposition and fun attitude *with them* when they walk in the door, the beneficial outcome is the same. Simple acts of laughter and humor can be accomplished in the workplace during breaks and meals. Being mindful of the little details throughout the day and how one's body is reacting to stressors can provide peace of mind and allow one to escape to a "fun place" in their mind.

Practicing the MAC Model throughout the workday can help facilitate vicarious fun/mental escapism and reduce workplace stress:

- Observe subtle humorous nuances present in the workplace and acknowledge the moment that you make each observation.
- Pay full attention to the mannerisms, behaviors, and subtleties of those in the workplace and how you respond to these observations.
- Accept this moment without judgment and have fun with it.
- Make a conscious choice to allow this moment to have a positive impact on you and make you happy and others happy.

Be it within the workplace environment, at home or in a social setting, adults will dedicate a vast amount of time establishing new relationships or nurturing existing ones. Playfulness and playful communication allow adults to refine and continually develop their social skills, as well as remove barriers to improved communication and interaction with others.[53] Establishing an identity within a workgroup, school classroom, or at a family reunion can be facilitated with humor and laughter as this provides a bit of an "ice-breaker" and makes the person appear to be more welcome within the group.[54]

Play and laughter can be an effective tool for nurturing and healing relationships. Making a conscious effort to keep play and humor alive in a relationship can bring a level of resiliency to the relationship, open up intimacy, build trust[55], and foster a team spirit. This has application not only in personal relationships but also in workplace relationships.

Sharing play and humor creates connectivity (a sense of intimacy) between two people and helps define a solid, successful relationship as there is a positive bond that is built, which helps buffer against stress, disagreements, and challenging periods within the relationship.[56]

Here are some ideas of how laughter, positive humor (free of ridicule), and playfulness might help manage relationship conflict and add longevity:[57–59]

Humor promotes resiliency by taking difficult issues in stride and without anger.

- Gentle humor can be used to address sensitive issues.
- Playfulness and humor creates a bond between people.
- Laughter helps people loosen up and inspires more open-minded thinking.
- Playful settings disarm defensiveness.
- Inhibitions are released during periods of humor and laughter.
- Tension can be eased during a power struggle and help regain perspective.

# ACTIVITY: THORNS AND ROSES[60]

*"Some people grumble that roses have thorns; I am grateful that thorns have roses."*

—Alphonse Karr[61]

For this exercise consider the current challenges and stressors in your work/school day and also in a relationship (personal or otherwise). These are going to be considered your *thorns*.

Now think of how play, laughter, or humor has either diffused those challenges/stressors or provided you a positive distraction. These are your *roses*.

If these challenges/stressors were not diffused or you were not distracted, be prepared to articulate how play, laughter, or humor *could* have been employed to provide a positive outcome.

Example: "I could have done this or I should have thought of…"

*Susii/Shutterstock.com*

My work/school thorn is _____

_____

My relationship thorn is _____

_____

*Dragana Gerasimoski/Shutterstock.com*

My work/school rose is _____

_____

My relationship rose is _____

_____

*Michael C. Gray/Shutterstock.com*

# Late Adulthood— Time to Laugh and Play

Late adulthood may pose increased potential of experiencing unique debilitating and disabling disorders due to advanced age and pre-existing medical conditions. Unfortunately, Alzheimer's disease is the most common neurodegenerative disorder and depression the most common affective disorder among older adults. Although many therapies exist to treat these disorders, laughter has shown itself to be an effective complementary therapy to improve mood and depression in these patients.[62]

Even for those not diagnosed with a specific medical condition, laughter therapy demonstrates the opportunity to reduce the incidence of insomnia and improve sleep quality in the elderly.[63] Some older adults may face physical or situational constraints that may limit their ability to participate in playful activities. This does not mean they cannot reap the mental and physiological benefits because, as was discussed earlier, "playtime" is any activity for pleasure that has no intended goal, formality, or serious purpose. Therefore some low-key, low-impact playful activities that can elicit a smile or perhaps even some laughter could be:

- Going to a park or family recreation area and watching children play or even just people-watching may not only add a smile to a face, but can help boost immunity because of the exposure to nature and the outdoors.[64]
- Simply going outside and participating in some ambulatory event, 30 minutes a day for a month, can increase happiness, energy levels, and improve sleep patterns.[65]
- Mindful engagement with nature's sights and sounds, as an observation or while playing an outdoor board game, can improve memory and cognitive function.[66]

Many older adults are healthy and not only enjoy playing but generally have more time to play and have fun. Engaging with family, especially grandchildren can bring a feeling of youthful enjoyment and feelings of connectedness.

The fact that people today are living longer has created an environment where organizations that focus on late adulthood travel and activities such as biking, hiking, adult education and social groups are becoming the norm.

Some older adults finally have the time to take up an instrument or sport, which can bring a feeling of accomplishment, defraying the possibility of loneliness, particularly when retirement brings more free time.

Simply stated, making time in our lives, whether young, old or in between, for play, laughter, and humor is the best medicine for connecting and forming relationships, increasing our immune system power, and bringing joy as well and purpose into our lives. We need food, water, air, and exercise to keep our bodies alive and play, laughter, and humor to keep our spirits alive!

Diego Cervo/Shutterstock.com

Monkey Business Images/ Shutterstock.com

arek_malang/Shutterstock.com

Alextype/Shutterstock.com

Warren Price Photography/ Shutterstock.com

# References

1. Oxford Edition Dictionary, O. E. (2011). Online version. Accessed February 26, 2015. http://www.oxforddictionaries.com/us/definition/american_english/smile

2. Lane, R. D. (2000). Neural correlates of conscious emotional experience. In R. D. Lane & L. Nadel (Eds.), *Cognitive Neuroscience of Emotion*. New York: Oxford University Press: 345–370.

3. Cannon, C. M., & Bseikri, M. R. (2004). Is dopamine required for natural reward? *Physiology & Behavior, 81*(5), 741–748.

4. Strathearn, L., Li, J., Fonagy, P., & Montague, P. R. (2008). What's in a smile? Maternal brain responses to infant facial cues. *Pediatrics, 122*(1), 40–51.

5. O'Doherty, J., Winston, J., Critchley, H., Perrett, D., Burt, D. M., and Dolan R. J. (2003). Beauty in a smile: The role of medial orbitofrontal cortex in facial attractiveness. *Neuropsychologia, 41*, 147–155.

6. Little, A. C., Jones, B. C., & DeBruine, L. M. (2011). Facial attractiveness: evolutionary based research. *Philosophical Transactions of the Royal Society of London B: Biological Sciences, 366*(1571), 1638–1659.

7. Karren, K. J., et al. (2010, p. 461). *Mind/Body health: The effect of attitudes, emotions and relationships*. New York, N.Y.: Benjamin Cummings.

8. Ekman, P., Davidson, R. J., & Friesen, W. V. (1990). The Duchenne smile: Emotional expression and brain physiology: II. *Journal of personality and social psychology, 58*(2), 342.

9. Hatfield, E., Cacioppo, J. T., Rapson, R. L., Clark, M. S. (Ed). (1992). Primitive emotional contagion. Emotion and social behavior. *Review of Personality and Social Psychology, Vol. 14*: 151–177. Thousand Oaks, CA: Sage Publications, Inc.

10. Wenk, Gary L., PhD. Your brain food: Can the simple act of smiling bring pleasure? *Psychology Today*. Retrieved at: https://www.psychologytoday.com/blog/your-brainfood/201112/addicted-smiling

11. Diggins, K. (2008). The power of a wmile. *Journal of Christian Nursing, 25*(3), 169.

12. Toda, M., Kusakabe, S., Nagasawa Skitamura, K., Morimoto, K. (2007). Effect of laughter on salivary endocrinological stress marker chromogranin A. *Biomed Research. 2007 Apr;28*(2):115–8.

13. Bennett, M. P. and Lengacher, C. Humor and Laughter May Influence Health: III. Laughter and Health Outcomes. *Evidence-Based Complementary and Alternative Medicine, vol. 5*, no. 1, pp. 37–40, 2008. doi:10.1093/ecam/nem041

14. Morse, D. R. (2007). Use of humor to reduce stress and pain and enhance healing in the dental setting. *J N J Dental Association. 2007 Fall; 78*(4):32–6.

15. Isenberg, J. P., & Quisenberry, N. (2002). A position paper of the Association for Childhood Education International PLAY: Essential for all children. *Childhood Education, 79*(1), 33–39.

16. McGhee, P. E., & Frank, M. (2014). *Humor and children's development: A guide to practical applications*. London: Routledge.

17. Frost, J. L. Neuroscience, play and brain development. (1998, June 18–21). Paper presented at: *IPA/USA Triennial National Conference* held at Longmont, CO. Retrieved at www.eric.ed.gov/ERICDocs/data/ericdocs2/content_storage_01/0000000b/80/11/56/d6.pdf

18. Hurwitz, S. C. To be successful: Let them play! *Child Educ.2002/2003;79*:101-102.

19. Isenberg, J., & Quisenberry, N. L. Play: A necessity for all children. *Child Educ.1988;64*:138–145.

20. Barnett, L. A. Developmental benefits of play for children. *J Leis Res.1990;22*:138–153.

21. Pellegrini, A. D., Boyd, B. (1993). The role of play in early childhood development and education: Issues in definition and function. In: Spodek, B., ed. *Handbook of Research on the Education of Young Children*. New York, NY: MacMillan:105–121.

22. Elias, M. J., Arnold, H. (2006). *The educator's guide to emotional intelligence and academic achievement: Social-emotional learning in the classroom*. Thousand Oaks, CA: Corwin Press.

23. Zins, J. E. (2004). Building academic success on social and emotional learning: What does the research say? New York, NY: Teachers College Press.

24. Rosenfeld, A. A., Wise, N. (2000). *The over-scheduled child: Avoiding the hyperparenting trap.* New York, NY: St Martin's Griffin.

25. Hallowell, E. M. (2002). The childhood roots of adult happiness: Five steps to help kids create and sustain lifelong joy. New York, NY: Ballantine Books.

26. Litt, M. D. (1996). A model of pain and anxiety associated with acute stressors: Distress in dental procedures. *Behaviour Research and Therapy, 34*(5), 459–476.

27. Marcon, M. (2005). *Humour for good health in The Emergency Department & Child and Adolescent Health Unit* (The Clown Doctor project). Victoria Australia: The Northern Hospital.

28. Meisel, V., Chellew, K., Ponsell, E., Ferreira, A., Bordas, L., & Garcia-Banda, G. (2010). The effect of "hospital clowns" on psychological distress and maladaptive behaviours in children undergoing minor surgery. *Psychology in Spain. 2010;14*(1):8–14.

29. Nevo, O., & Shapira, J. (1989). Chapter 8: The Use of Humor by Pediatric Dentists. *Journal of Children in Contemporary Society, 20*(1–2), 171–178.

30. Pellegrini, A. D. (1995). *The future of play theory: A multidisciplinary inquiry into the contributions of Brian Sutton-Smith*. SUNY Press.

31. Aamoth, D. (2014, May 27). Here's how much time people spend playing video games. *Time.* Retrieved from http://time.com/120476/nielsen-video-games/

32. The Neilsen Company. (2013). *The teen transition: Adolescents of today, adults of tomorrow.* New York, NY: The Neilsen Company. Retrieved from http://www.nielsen.com/us/en/newswire/2013/the-teen-transition--adolescents-oftoday--adults-of-tomorrow.html

33. Plancherel, B., & Bolognini, M. (1995). Coping and mental health in early adolescence. *Journal of Adolescence, 18*(4), 459–474.

34. Berger, B. G., Friedmann, E., & Eaton, M. (1988). Comparison of jogging, the relaxation response, and group interaction for stress reduction. *Journal of Sport and Exercise Psychology, 10*(4), 431–447.

35. beta-endorphins. (n.d.) *Segen's Medical Dictionary*. (2011). Retrieved from http://medical-dictionary.thefreedictionary.com/beta-endorphin

36. catecholamine. (n.d.) *Mosby's Medical Dictionary, 8th edition*. (2009). Retrieved from http://medical-dictionary.thefreedictionary.com/catecholamine

37. Brown, M. R., Fisher, L. A., Spiess, J., Rivier, C., Rivier, J., & Vale, W. (1982). Corticotropin-releasing factor: Actions on the sympathetic nervous system and metabolism*. *Endocrinology, 111*(3), 928–931.

38. Hasan, H., & Hasan, T. F. (2009). Laugh yourself into a healthier person: A cross cultural analysis of the effects of varying levels of laughter on health. *Int J Med Sci, 6*(4), 200–11.

39. Berk, L. S., Tan, S. A., Fry, W.F. (1993). Eustress of humor associated laughter modulates specific immune system components. *Annals of Behavioral Medicine:* 15:11.

40. Bressler, E. R., Martin, R. A., & Balshine, S. (2006). Production and appreciation of humor as sexually selected traits. *Evolution and Human Behavior, 27*(2), 121–130.

41. Campbell, L., Martin, R. A., and Ward, J. R. (2008), An observational study of humor use while resolving conflict in dating couples. *Personal Relationships, 15*:41–55. doi: 10.1111/j.1475-6811.2007.00183.x

42. Vela, L. E., Booth-Butterfield, M., Wanzer, M. B., & Vallade, J. I. (2013). Relationships among humor, coping, relationship stress, and satisfaction in dating relationships: Replication and extension. *Communication Research Reports, 30*(1), 68–75.

43. Strean, W. B. (2008). 13. Evolving toward laughter in learning. *Collected Essays on Learning and Teaching, 1*, 75–79.

44. Hovelynck, J., & Peeters, L. (2003). Laughter, smiles and grins: The role of humor in earning and facilitating. *Journal of Adventure Education & Outdoor Learning, 3*(2), 171–183.

45. Weeks, M. (2012). Comic theory and perceptions of a disappearing self. 34(1), 19–29. Weeks, M. (2012). Comic Theory and Perceptions of a Disappearing Self. 言語文化論集, *34*(1), 19–29. Translated from a Japanese Publication

46. Rockman, I. F. (2003). Fun in the workplace. *Reference Services Review, 31*(2), 109–110.

47. Saad, L. (2014). The "40-hour" workweek is actually longer—by seven hours. *Gallup. Available online at http://www.gallup.com/poll/175286/hour-workweekactually-longer-seven-hours.aspx*

---

48. Geurts, S., & Grundemann, R. (1999). Workplace stress and stress prevention in Europe. In M. Kompier & C. Cooper (Eds), *Preventing stress, improving productivity: European case studies in the workplace*, 9–33. London: Routledge.

49. Fry, A. (2004). *Laughing matters: The value of humor in the workplace*. Krug Industries, Inc. Better Way Press

50. Bureau of Labor Statistics, U.S. Department of Labor. (2015). Illness-related work absences in January2015. *The Economics Daily*. Retrieved from http://www.bls.gov/opub/ted/2015/illness-related-work-absences-in-january-2015-littledifferent-from-a-year-earlier.htm

51. McEwen, B. S. (2008). Central effects of stress hormones in health and disease: Understanding the protective and damaging effects of stress and stress mediators. *European Journal of Pharmacology, 583*(2), 174–185.

52. Jacobson, B. H., Aldana, S. G., Goetzel, R. Z., Vardell, K. D., Adams, T. B., & Pietras, R. J. (1996). The relationship between perceived stress and self-reported illness-related absenteeism. *American Journal of Health Promotion,11*(1), 54–61.

53. Mount, M. K. (2005). Exploring the role of self-disclosure and playfulness in adult attachment relationships. http://hdl.handle.net/1903/2928

54. Fine, G. A., & Soucey, M. D. (2005). Joking cultures: Humor themes as social regulation in group life. *Humor-International Journal of Humor Research, 18*(1), 1–22.

55. Aune, K. S., & Wong, N. C. (2002). Antecedents and consequences of adult play in romantic relationships. *Personal Relationships, 9*(3), 279–286.

56. Martin, R. A. (2007). *The psychology of humor: An integrative approach.* Ontario: Elsevier Academic Press.

57. Butzer, B., & Kuiper, N. A. (2008). Humor use in romantic relationships: The effects of relationship satisfaction and pleasant versus conflict situations. *The Journal of Psychology, 142*(3), 245–260.

58. Rust, J., & Goldstein, J. (1989). Humor in marital adjustment. *Humor-International Journal of Humor Research, 2*(3), 217–224.

59. De Koning, E., & Weiss, R. L. (2002). The relational humor inventory: Functions of humor in close relationships. *American Journal of Family Therapy, 30*(1), 1–18.

60. Din, E., Kelly, S., Nelson, D., *Gateway to Holistic Healing* Emory University, Nell Hodgson Woodruff School of Nursing.

61. Karr, A., Harvey, W., & Leighton, J. (1855). *A tour round my garden.* London: G. Routledge & Company.

62. Walter, M., Hänni, B., Haug, M., Amrhein, I., Krebs-Roubicek, E., Müller-Spahn, F., & Savaskan, E. (2007). Humour therapy in patients with late-life depression or Alzheimer's disease: A pilot study. *International Journal of Geriatric Psychiatry, 22*(1), 77–83.

63. Ko, H. J., & Youn, C. H. (2011). Effects of laughter therapy on depression, cognition and sleep among the community-dwelling elderly. *Geriatrics & Gerontology International, 11*(3), 267–274.

64. Park, B. J., Tsunetsugu, Y., Kasetani, T., Kagawa, T., & Miyazaki, Y. (2010). The physiological effects of Shinrin-yoku (taking in the forest atmosphere or forest bathing): Evidence from field experiments in 24 forests across Japan. *Environmental Health and Preventive medicine, 15*(1), 18–26.

65. David Suzuki Foundation 30 x 30 Nature Challenge. Retrieved from http://www.davidsuzuki.org/media/news/2013/07/report-confirms-daily-dose-of-natureboosts-happiness-wellbeing/

66. Berman, M. G., Jonides, J., & Kaplan, S. (2008). The cognitive benefits of interacting with nature. *Psychological Science, 19*(12), 1207–1212.

## CHAPTER 4 QUESTIONS

1. What is the definition of play?

2. What is a "Duchenne" smile and what makes it unique to any other type of facial expression?

3. In studies related to adolescents, laughter decreased three particular stress hormones and fortified the activity of the natural killer (NK) cells effectively keeping the immune system strong. What were these stress hormones?

4. List some examples of how children's hospitals, pediatric wards, and pedodontic offices are incorporating playfulness and humor to help reduce anxiety and promote wellness in children:

5. How does maintaining an appropriate level of fun and humor in the classroom benefit students?

6. What are some ways in which humor/laughter can help build longevity and manage relationship conflict?

7. Among older adults, what is the most common neurodegenerative disorder and what is the most common affective disorder?

# MINDFUL AWARENESS REFLECTION JOURNAL

4 Step **MAC** Guide

Choose one mindful experience as you begin your reflection.

## Empathically Acknowledge

Describe your experience.

_____

_____

_____

## Intentional Attention

Describe what you noticed.

| Breath | |
|---|---|
| Body | |
| Emotions | |
| Thoughts | |
| Senses | |

## Accept Without Judgment

Describe judgment; acceptance.

_____

_____

_____

## Willingly Choose

Choose to purposely respond to your experience.

_____

_____

_____

## Mindful Mac Meditation

Describe your meditation experiences. What did you learn from your meditation experience?

_____

_____

_____

# Mindful Daily Journal

_TODAY'S Insight NOW!_

_Tips for Wellbeing_
- _Have Hope_
- _Accept Yourself_
- _Exercise_
- _Practice Mindfulness_
- _Express Gratitude_
- _Master Your Environment_
- _Find Purpose_
- _Stay Connected_
- _Be an Optimist_

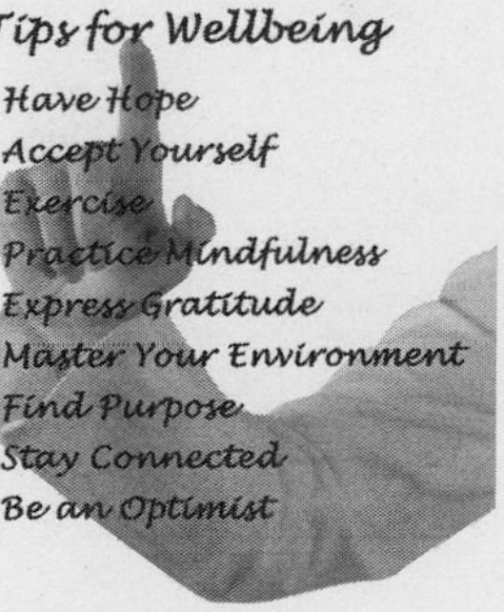

Date: _____     Make Today Count!

# CHAPTER 5

# Healthy Relationships Across the Lifespan

**Tamara Rounds**

*Photo courtesy of Maria Napoli*

*What is love?*
*Gentle touches*
*Safety*
*Trust*
*Being heard*
*Unconditional acceptance*
*This is love*

Maria Napoli

Andresr/Shutterstock.com

Let's begin this chapter by taking a moment to write down all your daily activities that involve another person.

1.

2.

3.

4.

5.

6.

What did you discover?

Does the number of activities you do that include interactions with another person surprise you?

Did you consider driving or commuting? You may think you are alone in your car or on public transportation, but did you consider that you are forming relationships with every car on the road while driving (presenting as the type of driver you are, your lane preference, your desired speed, communicating through your horn, hand gesture, cutting another driver off, using your blinker) or every new person who decides to take a seat or stand next to you on the bus (navigating your physical space with another individual, avoiding eye contact with the person sitting next to you, reading, closing your eyes, wearing earbuds, placing your packages in the space next to you so someone can't occupy the space)? Whether you speak or not, you are forming some kind of relationship with other drivers or commuters.

Did you stop to consider you navigate a new relationship every time you stand in line at the grocery store checkout, or wait for the food server to bring your meal?

Amazing, isn't it that we take for granted how much of our daily energy is focused on navigating interpersonal relationships?

It's incredible how little attention we pay to creating relationships with everyone we encounter. Conversely, how much time do you spend preparing to be the best person you can be in a relationship? Yet, we know *it is the relationships among ourselves and others that have the most influence in our lives towards happiness.* Humans are hardwired to connect and be with others. Human connection and intimacy are necessary if we are to thrive as individuals. John Bowlby, a British psychologist, psychiatrist, and psychoanalyst noted for his research in child development and for his pioneering work in attachment theory, argues that our need to bond with others is more fundamental to basic needs then our physiological requirements.[1,2,3]

Current research in positive psychology suggests our happiness depends on our success in the environment and in social interpersonal relationships.[4] Brene Brown in her book *The Gifts of Imperfection* defines the human connection "as the energy that exists between people when they feel seen, heard, and valued; when they can give and receive without judgment; and when they derive sustenance and strength from the relationship."[5]

The dictionary defines a relationship as "the way in which two or more concepts, objects, or people are connected."[6] Humans are vertebrates of the mammalian classification often referred to as mammals. Mammals are known for living in groups or families as a means of survival. There is safety in numbers and having several individuals on the lookout for danger or assisting in gathering and sharing food with one another has contributed to the evolution of our species and not our extinction. Being in relationships with others is hardwired into our anatomy.[7]

Your very existence began with two people having a sexual relationship with one another. You are here today reading this chapter because of that relationship. You may think by being in the womb meant you were totally separate from your mother, but in reality your relationship to your mother and your survival was completely dependent on her for everything: your cell development, your nutrition and food, and some research even suggest your personality and temperament.[8,9,10,11]

Researchers are investigating the attachment and neurobiological effects of experiences before, during, and after birth. Their findings suggest these first experiences prime a baby's brain and body responses for a lifetime. These early bonding moments forge what researchers believe are early personality development and nonverbal communication between the infant and mother. This environment sets the stage for attachment, which is imperative for survival in and out of the womb. Human beings differ from most mammal species by coming into this world helpless and dependent on others for our continuance. If we are ignored, isolated or disregarded by our caregivers we surely will die.[12,13,14]

You were completely dependent on your mother from the moment of conception. For example, if your mother experienced chronic stress before your birth, as an infant you were directly being exposed in the womb to your mother's neuro-hormonal and neuro-chemical status—called cortisol—through her bloodstream. High levels of cortisol for long periods of time affect the baby's hippocampus region of the brain. The hippocampus is part of the limbic system, the region of the brain that regulates emotion. The hippocampus is mainly associated with memory. In animal research, if the cells in the hippocampus region are remarked, it can lead to aggressive behavior and less socially co-operative behavior.[15]

In the womb you are already learning that other people's behaviors, actions, and choices are having a very significant impact on your ability to survive. You are learning almost immediately how to engage, build, and sustain relationships that will be required throughout your lifetime. *The case this author is making is that most of your time, on a daily basis, is spent being in relationships.* Forming and developing healthy relationships with others is fundamental for human development.[16] If you agree with this idea, why not consider becoming proficient in building strong relationships with those around you and reaping the benefits that healthy relationships inherently bring to your life? Why would anyone want to continue to perpetuate unhealthy, undesirable relationships, and experience the problems and outcomes that occur from being in unhealthy relationships with others?

## Relationships Through the Lifespan

We are in a relationship with someone ever since our conception. What happens to those relationships once we are born?

Within minutes of your first breath outside the womb you are already engaging in relationships with others. Think of how many hands touch you moments after birth. Some of those encounters are pleasant; some are not. Imagine how you may have reacted when your body, which never had a solid mass of any material ever touch it, was wrapped in a blanket for the first time. It probably didn't feel all

Nate Allred/Shutterstock.com

that comforting and loving. But let's not forget the good such as the first time your mother or father looked directly at your face and into your eyes or you felt the caressing touch of a person's hand. It wasn't too long before you realized you could not survive as an infant without the attention and care of others. Likewise, your parents undoubtedly realized they had a new, live, little being in their care and the enormous responsibility they felt for your feeding, daily care, and survival. Within minutes of your birth, your parents learned they needed to forge a relationship with you if you were going to survive.

In your early years as an infant you are totally dependent on your parents for most everything until you begin to navigate your own independence and chart your own growth and development. As a young child you begin to slowly explore your world by learning to walk and later by attending school. Your physical, emotional, and spiritual growth is very much contingent on your relationship with others. In middle and high school you begin to really expand your horizon and forge new frontiers with the focus of your development answering questions such as "Who am I?" The first two decades of your life generally focus on differentiating yourself from others and growing to become successfully independent and autonomous. You are always in relationships with others—parents, school friends, extended family, acquaintances. You are close to individuals who are unique to your social circles or hobbies, sports teams, group exercises in school, dating, and being affiliated to special interest groups maybe at church, school or in the community. You are continually learning who you are while maintaining certain independence as it relates to being in relationships with others.

Once you make a decision to choose a life partner, you make a commitment to that person, agreeing to compromise and work together not as separate units (as was the goal in the earlier developmental stages), but as a couple. You still maintain your independence, but now you need to learn to be a couple too. If you decide to have children, you now have to learn to accommodate even more individuals as you grow your family; each person being a separate individual yet also being part of the whole. When children grow their own independence and emancipate, your family unit will again downsize and make adjustments. As you near the end of your life you may find yourself once again alone, after decades of being a part of the whole, due to the death of your partner or other people departing who were part of the whole. The cycle of life comes full circle. Relationships through our lifespan are always in transition, changing, forging new frontiers, expanding, regrouping, and downsizing.

## ACTIVITY: WHAT YOU MUST KNOW TO SUSTAIN A GREAT RELATIONSHIP

Before reading the next section, watch the video below and reflect upon the types of relationships you are engaged in. The presenter draws inspiration from Steven Covey's relationship model of codependent, independent, and interdependent to discuss the psychology and ballet of a healthy relationship. (https://www.youtube.com/watch?v=XF77426aWzY)

You may find that there is a balance in the three types; maybe more focus on one or another. This is an opportunity to gain awareness. Describe below what is meant by:

Codependent

_____

_____

_____

Independent

_____

_____

_____

Interdependent

_____

_____

_____

## Characteristics of a Healthy Relationship

The Polyvagal Theory in essence states that mammals have a nervous system that begins functioning, organizing, and interpreting social behavior from the moment of birth; it exists to support us and communicate with the environment. In other words, we human mammals must determine friend from foe and evaluate whether the environment is safe for social engagement or decide if it is risky and prepare the body for emergency mobilization.[17]

Human beings are on a quest for *safety* and we use others (in reciprocity) to feel safe and calm. When we feel safe in relationships, we feel calm. The perception of safety is the turning point in the development of relationships. This perception is determined by our nervous system, which has a detection system capable of distinguishing situations that are dangerous or life-threatening or safe and amenable to being physically and socially approachable. If we feel unsafe, our brain sends a message to "flee—flight or fight" and we shut down because we identify risk factors that make it impossible for us to "trust" the other. [18] So turning our attention now to elements and qualities found in healthy relationships, let's explore the characteristics of a healthy relationship that allow us to feel safe and calm. After all, we are all living creatures living in relationships.

It stands to reason that a healthy relationship is based on equality and respect, not power and control. Here are a few common characteristics that are generally found in healthy relationships and how these qualities show up in the relationship.

| | |
|---|---|
| Honesty and Accountability | Accepting responsibility for one's self. Communicate openly and truthfully about your thoughts and behaviors without distortion, minimization, or blaming others. Admit mistakes if you are wrong. You keep your word and don't make excuses for others or for your actions. Relationship is built on truth and not manipulation, game playing, devious strategies, crafty tactics, or premeditative plans. |
| Transparent Communication | Being able to be candid and freely express your feelings, thoughts, opinions, reactions, and perceptions even if you know the other will disagree with you. Transparent communication is saying what you mean and meaning what you say. Knowing what your needs are and able to communicate them clearly, assertively with respect and mutual understanding. Communication is equal parts listening and speaking. |
| Negotiation, Compromise and Fairness | Ability to resolve conflict in ways that are mutually satisfying and agreeable to both. Both sides of the conflict are seen as valid and compromise means working to find mutually satisfying solutions that take into account both sides. |
| Trust and Support | Trust is earned; it is not automatic. Having "your partner's back" and wanting the best for them. Supporting their goals. Respecting other people's feelings, thoughts, and opinions. Valuing and believing in the other person for who they are and not what you want them to be. Entrusting, confiding, and feeling safe to share private aspects of yourself with them. |
| Respect | Accept others for who they are and value them for what they can bring to the relationship. Listen to one another without judgment. Being understanding and affirming each other even when their opinion is different than your own. Regarding the other person with courtesy and dignity. Accepting differences in one another and not demanding others need to change to meet your expectations. |
| Shared Responsibility | Making and sharing decisions together. Giving as much as you receive. |

| | |
|---|---|
| Shared Power | Equal say in the relationship. At times one person may appear to have more power than the other but it is eventually equalized between individuals. |
| Financial Partnership | Making financial decisions together with the idea of making sure both people benefit from financial arrangements. |
| Demonstrate non-threatening behavior | Talking and acting in ways that both individuals feel safe and not attacked verbally, emotionally, or physically. Neither person in the relationship should have control or use their temper to keep the other in line. Willingness to let down your barriers and allow the other person to see your weakness without fear of negative reactions or retaliation. |
| Intimacy | Respecting your partner's boundaries and honoring their request to set limits. Paying attention to each other's need for privacy. Not pressuring someone to act in ways they feel uncomfortable. Asking before acting. |
| Integrity | Being faithful and loyal when in a committed relationship. Upholding goodness in the relationship with sincerity and virtue that is true to your moral principles and shared by your partner. |
| Empathy | Being able to see things from the other's point of view. You don't necessarily need to agree with their point of view but you do need to work towards understanding it. |
| Love and respect yourself enough to know your limits and contributions | No one person can meet all your needs and expectations. It is okay to have different friends who meet different needs outside of the relationship. |
| Loyalty and Sincerity | There should be no question of your commitment to make this relationship work. Say what you mean and mean what you say. Your words are backed up by your actions and behaviors. |
| Compassion and Empathy | Can I place myself in the others shoes and have genuine concern for the issues they are concerned about? |
| Consideration | Being able to consider what the other person's needs are as well as my own. |
| Compatibility and Enjoyment | Sharing and valuing time together. Laughing with one another and enjoying each other's company. Taking interest in each other's lives: family, friends, clubs, school, interests. |

*Adapted from www.campbell.edu*

We all have human needs that are universal regardless of culture, gender, age, or place of origin. Most all of these needs can be satisfied in our relationships with others.

We all have the need to *connect*.[19] Under connection some common needs are:

| | | |
|---|---|---|
| Acceptance | Affection | Appreciation |
| Authenticity | Care | Communication |
| Companionship | Consideration | Empathy |
| Inclusion | Intimacy | Love |
| Nurturing | Presence | Respect/Self respect |
| Security | Self-acceptance | Stability |
| Support | Trust | Understanding |

We all have needs to *play*.[20] Under play some common needs are:

| | | |
|---|---|---|
| Adventure | Excitement | Fun |
| Humor | Joy | Relaxation |
| Stimulation | "Flow" | Spontaneous |

We all have needs of *physical well-being*.[21] Some common needs under physical well-being include:

| | | |
|---|---|---|
| Air | Care | Comfort |
| Food | Rest/sleep | Protection/safety |
| Shelter | Touch | Water |

We all have a need to have *meaning in our life*.[22] Under this category some common themes are:

| | | |
|---|---|---|
| Celebration | Challenge | Competence |
| Consciousness | Contribution | Discovery |
| Efficiency | Growth | Integration |
| Integrity | Learning | Progress |
| Self-expression | Stimulation | Understanding |

We all have needs to have *self-determination*.[23] Under self-determination some common needs are:

| Choice | Dignity | Freedom |
|---|---|---|
| Independence | Self-expression | Space |
| Spontaneity | Privilege | Relief from pain |
| Self-reliance | Self-determination | Discourse |

*Adapted from www.trf.net*

We just explored the characteristics of healthy relationships—qualities that register in our brain as being "safe" and allow us to connect, trust, and build connections that promote our best interest and promote our survival. But what does an unhealthy relationship look like? You oftentimes know you are in an unhealthy relationship when you walk away from someone and feel really bad about yourself; not once but again and again, time after time. You don't feel safe. You are always looking over your shoulder or have a feeling of needing to be "on guard" just in case. Another red flag that indicates you are in an unhealthy relationship is when you are called names that are unpleasant or others try and manipulate you or make you do something you don't want to do. Fear is a big warning sign. You are afraid to say what you think, to express your feelings without expecting retaliation or you find yourself "walking on eggshells" because you fear how the other person will react to you. Pushing grabbing, hitting, punching, or throwing objects are common in unhealthy relationships. Another example of being in an unhealthy relationship occurs when your partner controls you by having all the money or resources; you are dependent on them for everything (transportation, where you work or maybe don't work, the friends you want to hang out with, who you see and can't see in your family). They may also threaten to harm you, your children, pets, and objects that have personal value to you. Unhealthy relationships oftentimes express themselves with blackmail, threats, or ultimatums. All of this registers in our nervous system, and ultimately in our brain as "run for your life."

## ACTIVITY: THE ULTIMATE TEST FOR A HEALTHY RELATIONSHIP

Before you read the next section, take a moment to reflect upon the healthy relationships you may or may not be in. Matthew Hussey asks you to consider some very compelling questions that will certainly help you answer questions about being in a healthy relationship. https://www.youtube.com/watch?v=LoYHoAH9gZE

Describe one or more relationships that you view as positive.

_____

_____

_____

_____

How does the relationship or relationships you just described make you feel?

_____

_____

_____

If you are not engaged in a positive relationship, what would you like to experience if you had one?

_____

_____

_____

_alphaspirit/Shutterstock.com_

In the next section we will explore what occurs in an unhealthy relationship. Take time to think about the people in your life and the impact they have upon your emotions, time, energy, physical body and, in general, your overall quality of life.

## ACTIVITY: EIGHT SIGNS OF A RELATIONSHIP GONE HORRIBLY WRONG

In this exercise, take a moment and reflect upon whether or not one or more of your relationships exhibits one or more of the warning signs that signal the relationship you are in is unhealthy. Before you complete the exercise read the following. http://www.upworthy.com/8-warning-signs-of-a-relationship-gone-horribly-wrong?c=upw1

| WARNING SIGN | PERSON(s) | HOW I FEEL | HOW I BEHAVE | HOW CAN I CHANGE? |
|---|---|---|---|---|
| Intensity | | | | |
| Jealousy | | | | |
| Control | | | | |
| Isolation | | | | |
| Blame | | | | |
| Criticism | | | | |
| Anger | | | | |
| Sabotage | | | | |

# Impact of Unhealthy Boundaries

Unhealthy boundaries usually send an alarm to proceed with caution or to stop altogether. Another alarm to look for is feeling drained or overwhelmed after spending time with that person. Unhealthy boundaries can include suddenly becoming intimate on the first meeting or telling the person too much personal information before you have determined they are safe and capable of respecting your vulnerability. Preoccupation with someone, stalking, or feeling overwhelmed by a person's constant attention is another sign your boundaries are unhealthy. If your friend always calls you to just "dump" or "vent" their problems to you without allowing you to reciprocate, then you might want to set a healthier boundary by saying "Hey, I keep noticing the only thing we have in common is you calling me whenever something is not working out for you and all you want is to dump your problems onto me. This arrangement is not working out for me and we need to change this dynamic between us if we are going to stay friends." What is important in establishing boundaries is that we communicate them to the other person! If you receive backlash from communicating your boundaries to someone or feel guilty, shameful for speaking up, or disrespected, it's best to just walk away and focus on some self-care or other relationships you have that are rewarding. Doing this establishes a boundary with that person that you are not willing to engage in "drama" at the cost to yourself.

If healthy relationships are based on genuine love, openness, vulnerability, and freedom to give oneself to another, unhealthy relationships are just the opposite.

Some common qualities of unhealthy relationships include:

| Abuse: sexual, physical and emotional | Power imbalance | Dishonesty |
|---|---|---|
| Distrust | Fear | Control |
| Secrecy | Selfishness | Shame |
| Unexpressed feelings | Unhappiness | Unresolved conflict |
| Guilt | Preoccupation with someone (stalking) | Loss of "self" |
| Loss of control | Physical hitting, punching or throwing objects | Threats to harm you |
| Victimization | Sacrificing "self" | Being violated |
| Tiptoe around unmentionable subjects or topics | Robbing of your identity | Smothered |

# Boundaries and Self-Care Throughout Your Lifespan

Every healthy relationship has boundaries. Boundaries tell us where *you* stop and I begin.[24] Effective boundaries are vital to healthy relationships. We need to learn how to establish boundaries with other people and find a balance in doing so. Creating weak boundaries with others could encourage them to take advantage of us, ignoring our personal space and limits. Establishing boundaries that are too rigid could cause people to see us as distant and unavailable. Setting boundaries takes practice and perseverance.

Using the example of owning a large plot of land, visualize your house being surrounded by forests, lakes, and other property owners. Every piece of land has established property boundaries; actual physical demarcations identifying your property to others. Healthy relationships have boundaries as well. Some boundaries are non-negotiable. An example of a non-negotiable boundary is intruding sexual advances (touching a person without asking or getting permission). Other boundaries are negotiable such as when a senior in high school hears he was accepted to the college of his choice and wants a "high five" slap as a way to congratulate and validate his hard-earned success. Weak or leaky boundaries in relationships happen when we become so enmeshed, so consumed by the other person's thoughts, actions, or ideas that we lose ourselves completely. We can't recognize our own feelings or separate ourselves from the other person.

Murray Bowen, a family psychotherapist, pioneered studies focused on family relationships and specifically transgenerational relationships or current family patterns and problems that tend to repeat over generations. His theory asserts that in order to have a healthy relationship and establish a strong sense of individuation one develops a "differentiation of self" or else a person finds themselves in a state of emotional fusion with members in their family of origin. Differentiation refers to a person's ability to distinguish him/herself from their family of origin on a personal and intellectual level. Bowen terms differentiation of self as the ability to function autonomously yet remain connected to important relationships. Emotional fusion on the other hand, is at the opposite end of this spectrum and implies emotional dependence. Individuals who find themselves fused in dependent relationships with others react emotionally without being able to think or act independently in the relationship. Individuals in highly-fused relationships often times experience high anxiety and fear of being rejected or that their decisions may cause emotional separateness.[25,26]

Healthy boundaries allow us to differentiate from one another and be in line with what our feelings, thoughts, and needs are in the relationship. Healthy boundaries separate our experiences from other people's experiences. When you live mindfully and with awareness you begin to feel more in control of yourself and are less likely to get caught up in other people's problems so much so that you treat their problems as your own. Creating health boundaries allows us to take better care of ourselves on all levels—emotionally, physically, mentally, and spiritually so we can experience and pay attention to our goals, desires, and needs throughout our lifespan. Remember we are hardwired to be in relationships—so make personal choices to be in healthy ones!

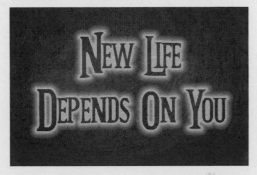

*Iliana Mihaleva/Shutterstock.com*

## ACTIVITY: SETTING BOUNDARIES

It may be difficult for you to set boundaries with people in your life. The following video illustrates positive straightforward guidance on boundary setting. The speaker pays particular attention to establishing boundaries with dysfunctional individuals and family members. Take a moment to reflect upon those people in your life with whom you have difficulty setting boundaries with after watching this video. https://www.youtube.com/watch?v=0AspHr5UCDA

Describe the person(s) in your life where boundaries are difficult to set.

_____

_____

_____

_____

Describe your behavior in this/these relationship(s).

_____

_____

_____

_____

Describe how you feel in this /these relationship(s).

_____

_____

_____

_____

What are you willing to do to make changes?

_____

_____

_____

_____

# The Adverse Childhood Experiences (ACE) study

Researchers from the Centers for Disease Control and Prevention (CDC) and Kaiser Permanente's Health Appraisal Clinic in San Diego embarked on one of the largest investigations ever conducted to assess associations between childhood maltreatment and health and well-being later in life. The Adverse Childhood Experiences (ACE) Study identified 10 ACE categories that include emotional, physical, and sexual abuse, emotional and physical neglect, witnessing domestic violence, growing up with mentally ill or substance abusing household members, loss of a parent, or having a household member incarcerated.[27]

The ACE Study demonstrated there is a strong relationship between the ACE Score and a wide array of health and social problems throughout the lifespan of an individual. More importantly, the ACE Study showed how childhood stressors affect the structure and function of the brain. Science from all fields is telling us strongly that we are not just social animals, but a type of animal who needs a close connection to others throughout our lifespan. *The quality of our relationships is a big factor in how mentally and emotionally healthy we are in our lives.* Many people experience harsh events in their childhood. Sixty-three percent (63%) of the people who participated in the study had experienced at least one category of childhood trauma. Over 20% experienced three or more categories of trauma referred to in the study as Adverse Childhood Experiences (ACEs). Here is what the study revealed:[28]

- 11% experienced emotional abuse.
- 28% experienced physical abuse.
- 21% experienced sexual abuse.
- 15% experienced emotional neglect.
- 10% experienced physical neglect.
- 13% witnessed their mothers being treated violently.

- 27% grew up with someone in the household using alcohol and/or drugs.
- 19% grew up with a mentally-ill person in the household.
- 23% lost a parent due to separation or divorce.
- 5% grew up with a household member in jail or prison.

"It is now clearly evident that ACE factors are common, highly interrelated, and exert a powerful cumulative impact on human development that becomes evident in problems across the lifespan."[29(p264)] Why is this study so important to you and the idea of relationships throughout the lifespan? The study suggests the more categories of trauma we experience in childhood, the greater the likelihood of experiencing:[30]

| | |
|---|---|
| Alcoholism and alcohol abuse | Fetal death |
| Depression | Illicit drug use |
| Poor health—related to quality of life | Risk for intimate partner violence |
| Liver disease | Sexually transmitted diseases (STDs) |
| Multiple sex partners | Obesity |
| Smoking | Unintended pregnancies |
| Suicide attempts | Ischemic heart disease (IHD) |
| COPD (Chronic Obstructive Pulmonary Disease) | ACESTUDY.org |

If we personally identify as having trauma and we experience some of the consequences of having traumas, we need to ask ourselves how this impacts our ability to have a healthy relationship with someone. Alcoholism, depression, illicit drug use, and partner violence directly impact our success at sustaining healthy relationships. Trauma can have broad and penetrating effects on an individual's personhood. Studies show that positive, loving connections with others protects us from stress, increases our immune system and helps us cope better through life's challenges. [31]

## Stages of a Healthy Relationship

In the beginning stages of building a relationship a lot happens. Initially, the honeymoon phase begins and everything appears to be exciting, amazing, and blissful. You can't believe the other person has everything you've always wanted and desire! Your chemistry is nothing short of being unreal. You can't wait to see this person again and the hours spent in the presence of this individual seem to fly by. During this stage it is important to enjoy the excitement and "natural high" you feel but also to keep in mind long-term relationships do need a solid foundation from which to grow. Focus on building that strong foundation by noticing the strengths and weakness of each other. Explore common interests you both enjoy and be open to expanding your horizons. Establish impeccable communication.

*Viorel Sima/Shutterstock.com*

So many things can influence the decisions and judgments we make. In this Science of Attraction video, Derren Brown, Kat Akingbade, and Charlie McDonnell investigate the Halo Effect and discover the impact it can have on first impressions and how others perceive you. https://www.youtube.com/watch?v=ZuometYfMTk. Explore your perceptions.

Describe what attracts you to others.

_____

_____

_____

Describe what you perceive makes others attracted to you.

_____

_____

_____

In the middle or working stage of a relationship there is a distinct transition. The honeymoon phase begins to fade and the realities and challenges present in daily life begin to surface. Situations such as work, the rearing of children, intimacy, sex, and work-life balance routinely impact what you want and what you need from a relationship. Changing expectations and personal goals are common and the need for couples to periodically check in with one another needs to be a priority. Disagreements are inevitable and healthy conflict resolution a priority. Common themes of conflict include career, marriage, unrealistic or unreasonable demands, issues involving behaviors of one partner or the couple, sex, extended family, outside pressures, decisions to start a family, parenting styles, and navigating the full spectrum of emotions that may include sadness, loss, tension, dishonesty, outright anger, disappointment, happiness, and feelings of love and satisfaction.

All relationships have a beginning, middle and an end. In the final stage of a relationship one or both parties leave the relationship. This can be voluntary (one or both decide to terminate the relationship out of choice such as in the case of a divorce) or involuntarily (one individual departs the relationship, leaving the other partner no other choice such as in the case of death).

To have healthy relationships we need to first pay attention to how we think, feel, and experience being asked, "What is a healthy relationship, and how would I define it?" Next, we need to look at some of the concepts that universally make for a healthy relationship. We need to take a deep breath and look inside ourselves for areas that need improvement, especially as they relate to having relationships with others. We know that happiness comes from our social relationships so becoming the best we can and improving our performance in relationships gives us the best shot at experiencing happiness throughout our lifespan. Some researchers have even suggested that "conscientious individuals" not only live healthier lives across multiple domains, but that people assessing mate preferences for long-term relationships tend to appreciate more those individuals whom they perceive as being conscientious because they are seen as working harder toward relationship success. [32,33]

The good news is that the human brain can develop—it is not static. The brain has plasticity—it does adapt, change, and evolve. The adult human brain can continue to grow, change, and grow neural connections and new neurons with each new experience even into old age![34] This is great news if you detected some ambivalence in yourself as you were reading this chapter, noticed patterns in your life that are healthy and unhealthy, or found yourself saying, "This is so me—I want this to change!" But how can you do this? Mindfulness, for example, has been shown to increase neuroplasticity. Your personal work in developing a daily mindfulness practice is significant in helping you adapt, change, and evolve.[35]

In summary, all people need connection to thrive. Meaningful interactions with others affirm we have purpose and a role in the world. We need to believe we make a difference in the world and our presence contributes to the overall understanding of everything that makes up our daily lives. There is growing evidence that close social relationships promote personal well-being throughout our lifespan. The capacity to form and maintain enduring interpersonal relationships is a hallmark of human development and personal satisfaction. There are benefits to individuals living a conscientious life that in particular predict healthier lives and greater success in their relationships with others. These are ideas that unite all of us regardless of our culture, experience, socio-economic status, gender, or age.

*Peshkova/Shutterstock.com*

# REFERENCES (Endnotes)

1. Bowlby, J. (1969). *Attachment and loss. Vol. 1. Attachment.* New York: Basic Books.

2. Bowlby, J. (1973). *Attachment and loss. Vol 2. Separation, anxiety and anger.* New York: Basic Books.

3. Bowlby, J., (1981). *Attachment and loss. Vol.3. Loss, sadness and depression.* New York: Basic Books.

4. Lopez, S. J., & Snyder, C.R. (2009). *The Oxford handbook of positive psychology, second edition,* Oxford: Oxford University Press.

5. Brown, B. (2010). *The gifts of imperfection.* Center City, MN: Hazelden.

6. Merriam-Webster (2015a). Merriam-Webster Online Dictionary. Retrieved from http://www.merriam-webster.com/dictionary/relationship

7. Janov, A. (2000). *The biology of love.* New York: Prometheus Books.

8. Klaus, M. H., & Kennell. J .H. (1982). *Parent-infant bonding.* St Louis: Mosby.

9. Odent, M. (2001). *The scientification of love.* London: Free Association Books.

10. Janov, A. (2001). *The biology of love.* New York: Prometheus Books.

11. Schore, A. N. (2003). *Affect regulation and the repair of self.* New York: W.W. Norton & Company.

12. Odent, M. (2001). *The scientification of love.* London: Free Association Books.

13. Klaus, M. H., & Kennell. J. H. (1982). *Parent-infant bonding.* St Louis: Mosby.

14. Klaus, M. H., Kennell, J. H., Robertson, S., & Sosa, R. (1989). Effects of social support during parturition on maternal and infant morbidity. *British Medical Journal:* 585–587.

15. *http://www.spiritualbirth.net/how-the-bowlby-attachment-theory-applies-to-pregnancy-and-birth*

16. Paat, Y. F. (2013). Relationship dynamics and healthy exchange across the family life cycle: implications for practice. *Journal of Human Behavior in the Social Environment,* no. (23) (2013): 938–953.

17. Porges, S.W. (2001). The Polyvagal Theory: Phylogenetic substrates of a social nervous system. *International Journal of Psychophysiology, no.* (42) (2001): 123–146.

18. Berceli, D. (2014). The joy of living in the parasympathetic system. In *Beyond stress strategies for blissful living.* Dubuque, IA: Kendall Hunt.

19. *www.trf.net.*

20. *www.trf.net.*

21. *www.trf.net.*

22. *www.trf.net.*

23. *www.trf.net.*

24. Katherine, A. (1991). *Where you end and I begin—How to recognize and set healthy boundaries.* New York: Parkside Publishing.

25. Haefner, J. (2014). An application of Bowen Family Systems Theory. *Issues in Mental Health Nursing* 35: 835–841.

26. Gubbins, C. A., Perosa, L. M., & Haring-Bartle, S. (2010). Relationships between married couples' self-differentiation/individuation and Gottman's model of marital interactions. *Contemporary Family Therapy 32* (2010): 383–395.

27. Larkin, H., Shields, J. J., & Anda, R. F. (2012). The health and social consequences of adverse childhood experiences (ACE) across the lifespan: An introduction to prevention and intervention in the community. *Journal of Prevention & Intervention in the Community* 40 (4) (2012): 263–270.

28. Centers for Disease Control and Prevention. *The adverse childhood experiences (ACE) study,* Retrieved from http://www.acestudy.org

29. Larkin, H., Shields, J. J., & Anda, R. F. (2012). The health and social consequences of adverse childhood experiences (ACE) across the lifespan: An introduction to prevention and intervention in the community. *Journal of Prevention & Intervention in the Community* 40 (4) (2012): 263–270.

30. Centers for Disease Control and Prevention. *The adverse childhood experiences (ACE) study,* Retrieved from http://www.acestudy.org

31. Larkin, H., Shields, J. J., & Anda, R. F. (2012). The health and social consequences of adverse childhood experiences (ACE) across the lifespan: An introduction to prevention and intervention in the community. *Journal of Prevention & Intervention in the Community* 40 (4) (2012): 263–270.

32. Hill, P. L., Nickel, L. B., & Roberts, B. W. (2014). Are you in a healthy relationship? Linking conscientiousness to health via implementing and immunizing behaviors. *Journal of Personality 82 (6) (2014):* 485–492.

33. Malouff, J. M., Thorsteinsson, E. B., Schutte, N. S., Bhullar, N., & Rooke, S. E. (2010). The five-factor model of personality and relationship satisfaction of intimate partners: A meta-analysis. *Journal of Research in Personality* (2010) 44, 124–127.

34. Garland, E., Howard, M. (2009). Neuroplasticity, psychosocial genomics, and the biopsychosocial paradigm in the 21st century. *Health and Social Work* August 34 no. 3 (2009): 191–198.

35. Berceli, D. (2014). The joy of living in the parasympathetic system. In *Beyond stress: Strategies for blissful living.* Dubuque, IA: Kendall Hunt.

## CHAPTER 5 QUESTIONS

1. True or false: Bowlby, a British psychologist. argues our need to bond with others is more funda-mental to basic needs then our physiological requirements.

2. Why are attachment and bonding moments during and after birth important to relationship development?

3. The Polyvagal Theory assumes all of the following EXCEPT:

   a. functions, organizes and interprets social behavior
   b. assists us to communicate with the environment
   c. automatically assumes everyone is a friend
   d. prepares the body for emergency mobilization

4. Discuss one common characteristic in a healthy relationship that you find particularly important. Why is it so important to you?

5. Healthy relationships are based on equality and respect not power and control. Why is this so important?

6. Describe examples of behaviors found in unhealthy relationships.

7. Why is the ACE (Adverse Childhood Experiences) study so important? How does trauma impact healthy relationships?

8. We are "hard-wired" to be in relationships with one another because:

   a. we need connection to other people in order to thrive
   b. relationships affirm we have purpose and a role in the world
   c. relationships promote personal well-being
   d. we need to believe we make a difference in the world
   e. relationships give us a sense of "safety" and "survival"
   f. all of the above

# MINDFUL AWARENESS REFLECTION JOURNAL

4 Step **MAC** Guide
Mindfully
acknowledge
attention
accept
choose

Choose one mindful experience as you begin your reflection.

### Empathically Acknowledge

Describe your experience.

_____

_____

_____

### Intentional Attention

Describe what you noticed.

| Breath |
|---|
| Body |
| Emotions |
| Thoughts |
| Senses |

### Accept Without Judgment

Describe judgment; acceptance.

_____

_____

_____

### Willingly Choose

Choose to purposely respond to your experience.

_____

_____

_____

### Mindful Mac Meditation

Describe your meditation experiences. What did you learn from your meditation experience?

_____

_____

_____

# Mindful Daily Journal

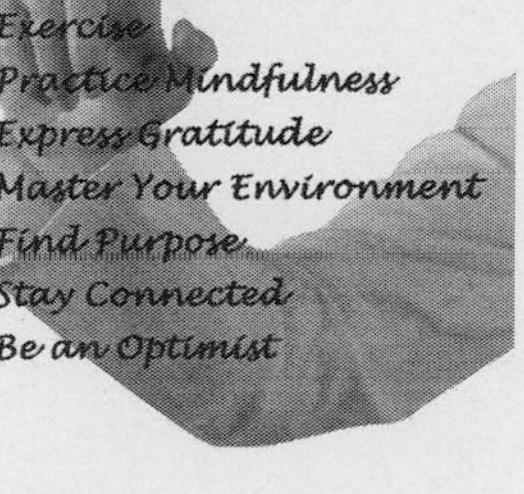

TODAY'S Insight NOW!

_____
_____
_____
_____
_____
_____
_____
_____
_____
_____
_____
_____
_____
_____
_____
_____
_____
_____
_____

*Tips for Wellbeing*

* Have Hope
* Accept Yourself
* Exercise
* Practice Mindfulness
* Express Gratitude
* Master Your Environment
* Find Purpose
* Stay Connected
* Be an Optimist

_____
_____
_____
_____

Date: _____ Make Today Count!

# CHAPTER 6
# The Benefits of Connecting with Nature

**Steve Peterson**

*Photo courtesy of Maria Napoli*

*Nature......*
*Alive*
*Simple*
*Exotic*
*Majestic*
*Nurturing*
*Always delivers*

Maria Napoli

*Photo courtesy of Maria Napoli*

Nature can be defined as a collective of the physical world, inclusive of the landscape, plants, animals, air, and those things not of human creation. Nature is the experience of one's senses while engaged in this collective through activities as wide-ranging as walking a dog, smelling the trees in a forest, feeling the rain upon one's skin, sitting on a beach, gardening, riding a skateboard or bicycling in a park, and photographing nature. The possibilities are endless but the underlying theme remains consistent: Take time to mindfully experience nature, and pay attention to the moment as it occurs.

Following are but a few examples of overt benefits of a healthy balance of human-nature interaction and connectivity:

Studies show the cognitive benefits such as skill development are enhanced in children with regular exposure to nature and the outdoors. Skills range from increased abilities in observation and creativity[2] to fostering language and collaboration skills when playground time is actually spent outdoors.[3]

Adult and adolescent intake of vitamin D, arguably challenging to get strictly from food as so few carry the vitamin naturally, is historically low and the prevalence of its deficiency is well-documented. The primary and ideal source is received from sensible sun exposure.[4]

Even for those limited in their ability to go outdoors (such as the elderly or home-bound), pictures of nature or other visual/sensory representations can help restore directed-attention and provide a level of mental comfort through a sort of "escapism" from the indoor environment.[5]

Colleges and universities have long integrated nature-awareness as a complementary component on campuses. Initiatives range from eco-friendly sustainability to open-air meeting areas, outdoor classroom environments, utilization of natural light and ventilation.

Employment of the four-step guide to mindfulness can open and enrich the experience of nature: 1) Acknowledging the moment in nature fully, 2) intentionally paying attention to that moment and opening the senses, 3) accepting all that nature offers to the senses without judgment, and 4) making a cognitive choice to allow nature to have a positive impact.

# Keep the Experience Simple and Manageable

Often when people think about connecting with nature, the assumption is that it must be a formal, structured activity. It is beneficial to attempt to redefine the concept of connecting with nature, for it does not have to be a holistic retreat on a mountainside or a Tai chi class in a grassy field. Although such activities are a marvelous way to discover nature's wonders and explore the unknown, sometimes too MUCH structure can take away from the magic of the mindful transformation, the personal connectivity, and inner exploration that nature has to offer in its simplest form!

*Photo courtesy of Maria Napoli*

If a generalized categorical statement about outdoor activity involvement across different periods of the lifespan were to be made, it would probably look something like this:

- Children require little structure; they are happy to be just playing outdoors.
- Adolescents form structure in their outdoor activities as it is a social/bonding event for them.
- Adults may require more structured events as they may have to be fit into their schedule. Such events may also act as a motivator to get them outdoors in the first place.
- Older adults may have more time to spend in nature, yet often are restricted due to increased medical issues and may experience the least amount of outdoor activity.

Removing the structure of an outdoor excursion allows for the experience to happen on its own terms and eliminates predisposed expectations. This also can reduce unnecessary complications and impediments to the outdoor experience, as well as increase participation from those who otherwise would not be able to be involved.

This can be likened to the family vacation that has an itinerary or sets times and points of interest. All energy is concerted on meeting preset deadlines and the focus is on the destination, not the trip itself and experiences in between.

It is important to be aware of the benefits of the more rudimentary and common outdoor activities such as taking a hike, doing outside chores, or even transplanting young basil from an indoor herb box to the moist soil outside your patio. At the time of planting the leaves of the basil are too small and immature to use. But you know that at the onset and still transplant it in anticipation of growth and *future* harvesting of the leaves. You have the patience. You watch your basil, nurture it, and appreciate its maturation process. You pay attention to the lighting, soil, and watering conditions as they will have an impact on the flavor of the basil. The journey of the growth of the plant makes the final outcome even more special. One can tailor the final outcome by paying attention to the little details along the way.

Mindfully engaging in basic outdoor activities can be more relaxing and less structured. Less structure leads to more mindfulness and more mindfulness leads to less stress.

# ACTIVITY: A PLANT IN YOUR LIVING SPACE

*"Bamboo is flexible, bending with the wind but never breaking, capable of adapting to any circumstance. It suggests resilience, meaning that we have the ability to bounce back even from the most difficult times."*

—Ping Fu[6]

Purchase a small indoor bamboo plant and a shallow container you can fill with water. This is a small investment with great longevity. Bamboo is suggested because it doesn't need soil and is easy to grow. All that is needed to maintain this plant is some sunlight and enough water to keep the roots/base covered.

Place it in an area of your living space that you will observe often. Observe it. Be mindful of your experience with this plant and absorb every detail and facet about its ability to thrive in nothing but water and some stones to keep it upright.

Write down five details about this plant as this is your first truly mindful encounter with it. Focus on specifics as if you are explaining this to someone who has never seen nor heard of a bamboo plant:

1. _____

_____

2. _____

_____

3. _____

_____

4. _____

_____

5. _____

_____

# Mental Roadblocks, Inattentiveness, and Mindfulness

I spent an afternoon with my parents recently and had an opportunity to make an observation about their three little dogs. Specifically, the difference between how the dogs acted while inside the house and their behavior once the door was opened and they discovered the back yard. Yes, I said *discovered* the back yard.

Phase4Studios/Shutterstock.com

At the time my parents had been living in this same house for nearly 20 years and the dogs were present for nearly eight of those years. These dogs have been familiar with this yard for a long time. Yet every time they went outside, they acted as if the entire landscape had changed from two hours prior and every blade of grass, every stick, every rock, every leaf, and every flower was brand new to them. Their noses were stuck in the air taking in every scent and aroma on the breeze, and then their heads would survey the ground with the greatest of attention and wonderment. Every little detail was exciting to them and caught their undivided attention. These dogs were re-discovering the back yard each and every time they went outside! Each time I watched this event unfold my immediate thought was "this has been the same back yard for nearly 20 years."

Gwoeii/Shutterstock.com

But it wasn't the same back yard for three little dogs who were excited to be outside and whose immediate response was to go into "discovery" mode. This "discovery" mode was not exhibited when they were in the house. They slept, casually played with the occasional toy, nibbled on food, and slept. But when that door opened a switch was flipped and they came alive.

My first thought was that these dogs live in a box … a house. They feel a level of comfort and security in that house, with its proverbial four walls and a roof. Their house-bound environment is structured and consistent and very safe for them. Yet when they run out the door into nature's wilderness they do not demonstrate any fear. For these dogs nature is not a box. It lacks structure and consistency and is ever-changing. Their exposure to nature lacks the moment-to-moment consistency that the safety and security of the house provides them. When they go outside they do not feel a lack of security; instead they are discovering the new and ever-changing environment. If anything, they appear to be more invigorated.

My second thought was, "Why don't people act as enamored with nature every time the door opens for them?"

In 2007 Gidlöf-Gunnarsson and Öhrström wrote that contact with nature impacted a person's psychological well-being by moderating daily "non-nature" processes such as daily structure, routine distractions, and disturbances. Specifically studied was that of community noise levels. It was suggested that the perceived availability of natural resources as a psychosocial outlet was negatively impacted by the level of noise and audible distractions[7]. This appears to be mostly an "adult" phenomenon, as children appear widely unaffected by urban noises when it comes time for them to play outdoors. However, studies suggest that children demonstrate improved levels of cognitive function when they are relocated from a concrete neighborhood landscape to one that contains more natural outdoor features (parks, greenery, etc.).[8]

This may be an underlying reason why many people do not embrace nature *by default*. If the moment one steps outside of their house and they feel overwhelmed by noise, activity, and other sensory overload, it is easy to understand why that would not elicit a cognitive and holistic sense of emotional "discovery"— a sense of calm.

A solution to this particular distraction may be as simple as redirecting the focus of attention. I like to refer to it as depth perception for the ears. Here is a very straight-forward exercise:

1. Go somewhere outside that has trees or water. A public or community park/recreation area is a good venue for this activity.

2. If there are some man-made noises present (people talking, music in the background, children playing, etc.) identify those noises.

3. Now concentrate on hearing nature's noises instead of the man-made distractive noises. Do you hear the birds? Do you hear the leaves rustling in the breeze? Do you hear the water from the water feature in the middle of the pond? Do you hear the ducks "honking" as they paddle around the water?

4. If there is no immediately available natural park feature, then simply walk somewhere outdoors and focus on *something* from nature. Smell a flower in a bush along the sidewalk, listen to the sprinklers watering a patch of grass, or even search for an aroma in the air.

"Let me know if I am distracting you."

This simple activity allows one to become mindfully aware of nature's surroundings instead of the distractions. It requires listening beyond the front noise and *discovering* the sounds in the background, an intentional attention to the background sounds.

I found myself doing this very thing one afternoon sitting on the patio of a restaurant waiting for a table to become available. The weather was warm with a slight breeze and there were dozens of birds in the trees in the immediate area. I became startled as the person whom I was with tapped me on the shoulder and said, "Didn't you hear them call your name? I went to the restroom and I heard them call you when I first walked in." I didn't even notice that she had walked away, let alone did I hear my name being called. I was too involved in the birds.

This is the same behavior my parents' three little dogs demonstrate when they are outside. When they are in discovery mode their names can be called two or three times and they fail to respond. It is not because they are ignoring the call as much as they are being distracted by being outdoors. Conversely, how often do people find themselves so distracted that they are *unable* to enjoy being outdoors?

To appreciate one's subconscious connection with nature it is first necessary to remove conscious distractions. Being mindfully attuned to the details of nature will help allow those distractions to fade into the background.

## ACTIVITY: OVERCOMING MENTAL ROADBLOCKS

*"I don't have a short attention span I just …*
*Oh, look, a squirrel!"*

—*ironydesigns.com*

Name three features of nature that exist just outside your literal or proverbial front door:

1. _____

2. _____

3. _____

Describe a natural scent/aroma that is in the air the moment you step out of your front door:

_____

_____

_____

List three reasons you do not have time to connect with nature:

1. _____

2. _____

3. _____

List three reasons how making time to connect with nature can benefit you:

1. _____

2. _____

3. _____

# Nature and Children: Time to Play

When thinking of a child, the first thought that pops into mind is that of play: running around, spontaneity, imagination, loud voices, and just having fun, acting upon whatever thought enters 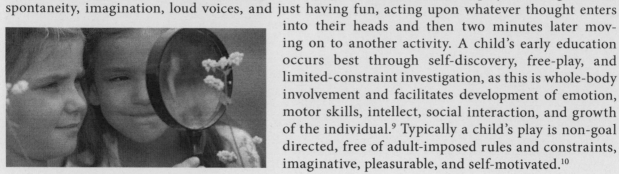 into their heads and then two minutes later moving on to another activity. A child's early education occurs best through self-discovery, free-play, and limited-constraint investigation, as this is whole-body involvement and facilitates development of emotion, motor skills, intellect, social interaction, and growth of the individual.[9] Typically a child's play is non-goal directed, free of adult-imposed rules and constraints, imaginative, pleasurable, and self-motivated.[10]

The concept of "wonder" has widely been accepted as a motivator for life-long learning.[11] Experiences children have when exposed to nature and outdoor environments have positive correlational links to the development of imagination and the sense of wonder.[12]

Unlike adults, who have grown accustomed to indoor environments (industrial, un-natural), children tend to respond more positively to outdoor experiences as they do not have this basis of comparison. As such children require a chance for solitude, contact with nature, and the "sense of wonder that nature offers."[12]

When comparing different environments for a child to play in, the sensory experiences are vastly different between indoor and outdoor, in addition to the obvious sets of rules and constraints that guide indoor activity. A child can be more free-spirited and has greater manipulation upon their outdoor environment versus an indoor area. In 1987, Elizabeth Prescott identified three traits that natural outdoor environments[13] offer for a child's arena of play:

- Unending diversity.
- Not created by adults (lacking adult rules and constraints).
- The feeling of timelessness (plants, trees, landscape, etc.).

The value that can be given to a child's outdoor play experience is similar to the values that adults hold about a natural outdoor environment: a place of exploration, rest and relaxation, rejuvenation, endless possibilities, and freedom from constraints and stress. Yet unlike an adult, children are free of that *value analysis*. They simply want to play and experience and discover without any underlying intent or goal.

To understand why children seem to demonstrate such a pronounced wanderlust for the outdoor world, one theory suggests that we were born with it. If this is the case, then this may help explain why natural environments play such a strong role in the child's learning process.

Biophilia is a theory that is gaining strong traction not only in the field of environmental psychology, but also in that of child psychology. The theory suggests that humans have a subconscious connectivity with nature and activities/objects in a natural surrounding.[14] Edward Wilson introduced the theory in 1984 and suggested that the bond with nature is instinctual with humans.[15] While this bond may be instinctual, it is refined and redefined over time through experience and is based on different cultures. This, too, may also explain why adults demonstrate infrequent and different levels of connectivity, whereas children participate in a universal mode of playfulness and engagement.

# Nature's Impact on Adolescent Development

The adolescent years are an incredible experiential and learning period. This is the point in our lives where we have flashes of intellectual brilliance and yet at the same time unregulated emotion. An adolescent is defining the world through intellectual and social discoveries. To fully appreciate the cognitive and social-developmental brain of an adolescent, it is important to understand the two opposing forces within the brain and how they develop as they do so at different stages and define the specific behaviors of the adolescent mind.

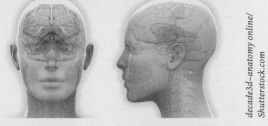

The Limbic System is the first to develop and is the center for instinctual and emotional reaction. Commonly referred to as "the social brain," this area is responsible for emotional impulses, selfishness, risk-taking behavior, and primitive motivation. This area of the brain does not change with time and is formative.

The Prefrontal Cortex is not fully matured until the early twenties and is the "reflective brain," where we find the hard-wired skills of thought differentiation, response inhibition, emotional regulation, prediction of outcomes, social control, and organization. This part of the brain is the "grey matter" that actually develops over time and is able to be formed by learning and experience[16]

Adolescents are very malleable and adaptive, yet they often have poor impulse control. They sometimes tend to be unaware of the implications their actions have on others and are constantly conflicted between their perception and the perception of others.[17] In short, the adolescent years (as we all remember) are a mentally and physiologically stressful period of development. Often an adolescent lacks the experience and coping mechanisms to make mindful, healthy decisions.

Research in environmental psychology has suggested that nature can provide a very adaptive function in the way of psychological restoration.[18] This restoration promotes not only a healthy outlook on situations and events, but also acts as a stress-relieving component. Interacting with nature can be a powerful tool to assist the adolescent through these tumultuous developmental years by allowing a "reset switch" to be thrown during periods of highly emotional activity and serve as a coping mechanism.

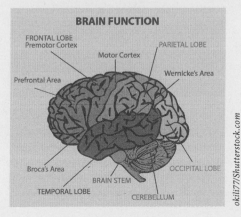

During this time period, there is also a tremendous explosion of synaptic growth that is unparalleled throughout the rest of our lives. Herein lies a window of learning opportunity that starts to close as we progress into adulthood. If lifelong environmental awareness and proactive behaviors toward ecological sustainability are to be developed, this would occur during the adolescent years where learning opportunity is at its greatest. Structured and residential learning activities held in outdoor settings have demonstrated a higher level of cognitive environmental awareness.[19] Such awareness will carry into and be evidenced/practiced in adulthood and ultimately passed onto the next generation.

The adolescent is also going through a period of defining self-identity. For many, their social world is cosmetically-driven through magazines, social media, movies, music, and peer-pressure. For others it is the influence of technology, video games, and urban industrialization. Nature can provide a radically different model of living that can help define an identity and sense of self in a more mindful and relaxed way that is free of structures, pressures, and expectations adolescents would normally be exposed to.

Research has found that adolescents tend to reflect metaphorically about natural features, animals, and landscapes to describe their moods, struggles, or need to establish a sense of identity.[20] Connectivity with nature can provide its own sense of stability and structure outside of the expectations and pressures associated with this challenging developmental period. A healthy influence of outdoor and nature exposure can provide a compensating balance for the adolescent.

## ACTIVITY: GROWING UP WITH NATURE

*"For human beings, habitat and environment are the literal space of the ground of thought ... The child is a 'traveler' mapping out the first spatially ordered reality of his life. The end of childhood is the end of that simple identity."*

—Paul Shepard[21]

| List your favorite indoor activities growing up | List your favorite outdoor activities growing up |
|---|---|
|  |  |

| Now list favorite indoor activities in your life right now | Now list favorite outdoor activities in your life right now |
| --- | --- |
| | |

Have your outdoor activities outnumbered your indoor activities?

Has there been a noticeable change from the number of outdoor activities as a child versus now?

## Adults Connecting with Nature: Time Constraints

Quite possibly one of the greatest impediments to adult interaction with nature or outdoor activities is the lack of available time. Or, more accurately, the perception of lack of available time or determination that connecting with nature should be a scripted, organized event.

The statistics of the American lifestyle support the notion that we are very busy and finding time to engage in outdoor activities is at a premium. Eighty-six percent (86%) of American males and 67% of American females work greater than a 40-hour work week.[22] Nearly one-third of those worked on weekends.[23] Forty percent of Americans report getting less than the recommended amount of sleep every day, averaging 6.8 hours when experts recommend seven to nine hours of sleep.[24] The U.S. Census Bureau reported that in 2010 of 45 selected leisure activities that adults participate in two or more times a week, only 13% of those activities were actually outdoor activities. The primary leisure activities were indoor activities that include socializing, watching television, and engaging in computer-assisted activities. This same report disclosed that from 2005 to 2010 there was a 15% reduction in the number of household lawn and garden activities engaged in by the American household.[25] To understand the comparison of activity level of adults to children and adolescents, The Outdoor Foundation reported in 2012 that nearly 50% of all American (age 6 and older) participated in outdoor recreational activities.[26] Drawing a loose correlation, this implies that there is a hypothetical 37% reduction in outdoor activity as we enter adulthood.

*auremar/Shutterstock.com*

Because adults have the busiest of schedules and the greatest level of personal, professional, and family responsibilities, it would stand to reason that the integration of an outdoor or natural experience would be one that takes this particular lifestyle into consideration. As mentioned previously in this chapter, keeping the experience with nature simple and manageable is an easy tool to integrate into a busy lifestyle.

To begin with, one of the basic reactions most people have when they engage with nature is to smell the environment and take it all in. This often results in a nice, full, deep belly breath. These big, refreshing, and rejuvenating full breaths pull air deep into the lungs and invoke the parasympathetic nervous system response. Blood is being fully oxygenated, the mind is clearing itself, the digestive system is mediating itself, and the body is working toward bringing itself into a homeostatic state. Homeostasis is the internal chemical stability, temperature regulation and pH balance as it responds to external stimuli.[27]

Simple outdoor chores, be it cleaning up an outdoor living space, mowing the lawn, landscape beautification, or watering flowers, require focus and full attention. This is mindful engagement. The mind is drawn away from any other task or thought and is focused on the present moment. Simple outdoor chores are, in effect, ongoing repetitive maintenance activities that the body finds relaxing and that relieve muscle tension (presumably due to muscle memory on otherwise consistent daily actions).[28]

Participating in a home-based horticultural activity is neither time-consuming nor expensive. Introducing a plant or seedling into a new environment is a truly mindful activity requiring great attention to detail and connection with the natural environment.

Gardening and grooming is nurturing new growth that could metaphorically serve as personal new growth. Activities such as these introduce us to brand-new scents, non-man-made textures, and the integration of the earth. We escape indoor contaminants and the familiarity of our everyday indoor environment. We escape the "autopilot" that we function within on a daily basis. When integrating ourselves with the earth, we have to be aware of brand-new details and sometimes brand-new environments. Not unlike going on a hike, every foothold is a new experience, requiring us to pay attention to small details and intricacies of a new environment. This redirected focus manages stress and anxiety by taking our minds away from other stressors.

As many adults lack sufficient sleep, bringing a natural environment into the sleep pattern may help produce a more restful night's sleep. Headaches, low oxygen saturation of the blood and mucous membrane, nasal and eye dryness and irritation are associated with poor room air ventilation, specifically, contaminated indoor air space.[29]

Whenever possible, opening a window where one sleeps can improve the air quality and be conducive to a more restful and productive night's sleep, as labored breathing is a major contributor to sleep apnea and other sleep disorders.[30] Approximately 18 million adults suffer from airway-related sleep apnea/sleep disorders according to the American Sleep Apnea Association. It makes sense to give our bodies fresh air as we sleep.

## ACTIVITY: FREE UP YOUR TIME FOR NATURE

*"Life will always get busy, make time to do the things you love"*

—Lailah Gifty Akita[31]

How many hours per day do you watch television or find entertainment on a computer/mobile device?

_____

_____

_____

_____

How many hours per week does that equate to?

_____

_____

_____

_____

How many hours per week do you spend actively engaging or interacting with nature?

_____

_____

_____

_____

Identify one unstructured outdoor activity that involves another person or a group of people that you would find pleasure in doing. What is it?

_____

_____

_____

_____

How much time, per week, would this activity involve?

_____

_____

_____

_____

## Older Adults and the Nature Connection

Older adults can face unique challenges, specifically mobility and accessibility, when it comes to engaging with nature. For those in long-term care facilities research has confirmed that time spent outdoors can improve their sleep patterns and ability to cope with pain as well as assist in recovery.[32,33] Outdoor areas of many facilities have been underutilized by the residents, and one of the primary reasons has been the landscape features, specifically, lack of seated areas comingled with trees and paved walkways to navigate through green areas. Residents reported an overwhelming desire to be outdoors versus indoors and cited the benefit as their "personal health." [34]

For those with limited mobility, one option to going outside to experience nature would be to bring nature *inside*. Bringing nature into a living space can provide the home-bound adult similar emotional and cognitive benefits as being outside. One easy transition would be the introduction of natural light and fresh air. Sunlight through a pane of glass and fresh air through an open window can elicit not only obvious health benefits but also help recall and recognition memories.[35] Such memories are comforting to elderly adults and may enhance transient cognitive function.

The introduction of house plants and providing care and nurturing of these plants has been shown to provide therapeutic and proactive care for patients with dementia. Contributing not only to maintenance therapy, but also improving quality of life.[36]

An artist's rendering of nature, be it a photograph, painting or picture, can stimulate cognitive processing. Placement of depictions of nature throughout one's living space can have soothing effects. Adults are enamored with the beauty and detail replicated through media, and although a media rendering cannot capture the smell of a tree or the way the leaves move in the wind, our own imagination can mindfully fill in those details.

In closing, here are some fast facts about how simple engagement with nature can have health benefits:

- Spending just 20 minutes a in a vegetation-rich environment improves vitality.[37]
- Living within one-half of a mile of a rich green space or wooded area decreases depression.[38]
- Exposure to plants and parks boosts immunity.[39]
- Spending 30 minutes a day in nature for 30 days can increase happiness, energy levels and improve sleep patterns.[40]
- Communing with nature inspires creativity.[41]
- Mindful engagement with nature's sights and sounds can improve memory and cognitive function.[42]

## References

1. Plath, S. (1971). *The bell jar.* New York: Harper & Row.

2. White, R. (2004). Young children's relationship with nature: Its importance to children's development & the earth's future. *White Hutchinson Leisure & Learning Group.*

3. Fjørtoft, I., & Sageie, J. (2000). The natural environment as a playground for children: Landscape description and analyses of a natural playscape. *Landscape and Urban Planning, 48*(1), 83–97.

4. Holick, M. F. (2010). *The vitamin D solution: A 3-step strategy to cure our most common health problems.* New York: Penguin.

5. Berman, M. G., Jonides, J., & Kaplan, S. (2008). The cognitive benefits of interacting with nature. *Psychological Science, 19*(12), 1207–1212. Smith, N. I. C. K. (2013).

6. Interview with CEO and founder of Geomagic Ping Fu. *Engineering & Technology, 8*(3), 64–67.

7. Gidlöf-Gunnarsson, A., & Öhrström, E. (2007). Noise and well-being in urban residential environments: The potential role of perceived availability to nearby green areas. *Landscape and Urban Planning, 83*(2), 115–126.

8. Wells, N. M. (2000). At home with nature effects of "greenness" on children's cognitive functioning. *Environment and behavior, 32*(6), 775–795.

9. Haas, M. (1996). Children in the junkyard. *Childhood Education, v72, n6, 1996,* Association for Childhood Education International, Wheaton, MD.

10. Hughes, F. P. (1991). *Children play & development.* Massachusetts: Allyn & Bacon.

11. Longworth, N. (1999). *Making lifelong learning work: Learning cities for a learning century.* London: Kogan Page.

12. Cobb, E. (1977). *The ecology of imagination in childhood.* New York: Columbia University Press.

13. Prescott, E. (1987). Environment as organizer in child-care settings. In C. S. Weinstein & I. G. David (Eds.), *Spaces for children: The built environment and child development.* New York: Plenum.

14. Fromm, E. (1964). *The heart of man.* New York: Harper & Row.

15. Wilson, E. (1984). *Biophilia*. Cambridge: Harvard University Press.

16. Popper, K. R., Eccles, J. C., John, C., & Carew, J. (1977). *The self and its brain* (Vol. 977, p. 362). Berlin: Springer International.

17. Pulkkinen, L. (1982). Self-control and continuity from childhood to late adolescence. *Life-span Development and Behavior, 4,* 63–105.

18. Van den Berg, A. E., Hartig, T., & Staats, H. (2007). Preference for nature in urbanized societies: Stress, restoration, and the pursuit of sustainability. *Journal of Social Issues, 63*(1), 79–96.

19. Bogner, F. X., & Wiseman, M. (2004). Outdoor ecology education and pupils' environmental perception in preservation and utilization. *Science Education International, 15*(1), 27–48.

20. Thomashow, C. (2002). Adolescents and ecological identity: Attending to wild nature. *Children and Nature: Psychological, Sociocultural, And Evolutionary Investigations*: 259–278.

21. Shepard, P. (1999). *Encounters with nature: Essays*. Washington, D.C.: Island Press.

22. Department of Statistics—International Labour Organization. www.ilo.org/stats.

23. https://www.bls.gov/news,release/atus.nr0.htm

24. https://www.gallup.com/poll/166553/less-recommended-amount-sleep.aspx

25. https://www.census.gov/compendia/statab/cats/arts_recreation_travel.html

26. https://www.outdoorfoundation.org

27. homeostasis. (2015). In *Encyclopædia Britannica*. Retrieved from http://www.britannica.com/EBchecked/topic/270188/homeostasis

28. Sempik, J., Aldridge, J., & Becker, S. (2005). *Health, well-being, and social inclusion: therapeutic horticulture in the UK*. Policy Press.

29. Finnegan, M. J., Pickering, C. A., & Burge, P. S. (1984). The sick building syndrome: Prevalence studies. *BMJ, 289*(6458), 1573–1575.

30. Rosen, C. L., D'Andrea, L. Y. N. N., & Haddad, G. G. (1992). Adult criteria for obstructive sleep apnea do not identify children with serious obstruction. *Am Rev Respir Dis, 146*(5 Pt 1), 1231–1234.

31. "Lailah Gifty Akita Quotes." *Lailah Gifty Akita Quotes (Author of Think Great)*. N.p., n.d. Web. 1 Feb. 2015. Retrieved at https://www.goodreads.com/author/quotes/8297615.Lailah_Gifty_Akita

32. Connell, B. R., Sanford, J. A., Lewis, D. (2007). Therapeutic effects of an outdoor activity program on nursing home residents with dementia. *Journal of Housing for the Elderly* 2007; 21(3/4):195–209.

33. Fujita, K., Fujiwara, Y., Chaves, P., Motohashi, Y., Shinkai, S. (2006). Frequency of going out-doors as a good predictor for incident disability of physical function as well as disability recovery in community-dwelling older adults in rural Japan. *Journal of Epidemiology* 2006; 16(6):261–270.

34. Rodiek, S. (2014). Access to *nature: Planning outdoor space for aging*. Center for Health Systems & Design. Texas A&M University.

35. Murphy, C., Nordin, S., & Acosta, L. (1997). Odor learning, recall, and recognition memory in young and elderly adults. *Neuropsychology, 11*(1), 126.

36. Chalfont, G. (2007). *Design for nature in dementia care.* London: Jessica Kingsley Publishers.

37. Selhub, E. M., & Logan, A. C. (2012). *Your brain on nature: The science of nature's influence on your health, happiness and vitality.* Hoboken, N.J.: John Wiley & Sons.

38. Being near nature improves physical, mental health. (2015, Feb. 1). *USATODAY.com.*

39. Park, B. J., Tsunetsugu, Y., Kasetani, T., Kagawa, T., & Miyazaki, Y. (2010). The physiological effects of Shinrin-yoku (taking in the forest atmosphere or forest bathing): Evidence from field experiments in 24 forests across Japan. *Environmental Health and Preventive Medicine, 15*(1), 18–26.

40. *David Suzuki Foundation 30 x 30 Nature Challenge.* Retrieved from http://www.davidsuzuki. org/media/news/2013/07/report-confirms-daily-dose-of-nature-boosts-happiness-wellbeing/

41. Study: Nature Inspires More Creative Minds. *MNN.* Retrieved from http://www.mnn.com/health/ fitness-well-being/stories/study-nature-inspires-more-creative-minds

42. Berman, M. G., Jonides, J., & Kaplan, S. (2008). The cognitive benefits of interacting with nature. *Psychological science, 19*(12), 1207–1212.

## CHAPTER 6 QUESTIONS

1.   What is the definition of nature?

2.   What is the four-step guide to mindfully experiencing nature?

3.   Give an example of a structured outdoor activity and an unstructured outdoor activity.

4.   What are three traits that natural outdoor environments offer children when they play?

5. Define *biophilia*.

6. What is the difference between the Limbic System and the Prefrontal Cortex?

7. According to the U.S. Census Bureau, what are the primary leisure activities that adults engage in?

# MINDFUL AWARENESS REFLECTION JOURNAL

Choose one mindful experience as you begin your reflection.

## Empathically Acknowledge

Describe your experience.

_____

_____

_____

## Intentional Attention

Describe what you noticed.

| Breath |  |
|--------|--|
| Body |  |
| Emotions |  |
| Thoughts |  |
| Senses |  |

## Accept Without Judgment

Describe judgment; acceptance.

_____

_____

_____

## Willingly Choose

Choose to purposely respond to your experience.

_____

_____

_____

## Mindful Mac Meditation

Describe your meditation experiences. What did you learn from your meditation experience?

_____

_____

_____

# Mindful Daily Journal

_____

_____

_____

_____

_____

_____

_____

_____

_____

_____

_____

_____

_____

_____

_____

_____

_____

_____

_____

_____

_____

*Tips for Wellbeing*

- Have Hope
- Accept Yourself
- Exercise
- Practice Mindfulness
- Express Gratitude
- Master Your Environment
- Find Purpose
- Stay Connected
- Be an Optimist

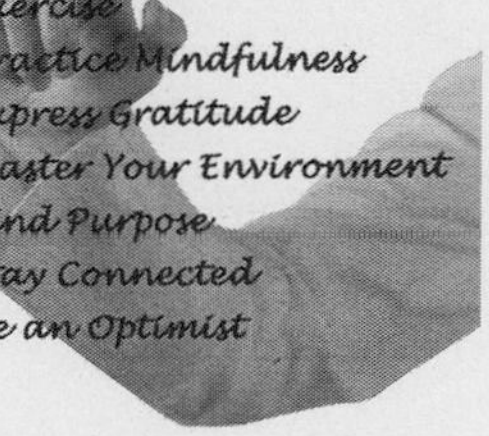

Date: _____     Make Today Count!

# CHAPTER 7

## The Benefits of the Human-Animal Relationship

**Steve Peterson**

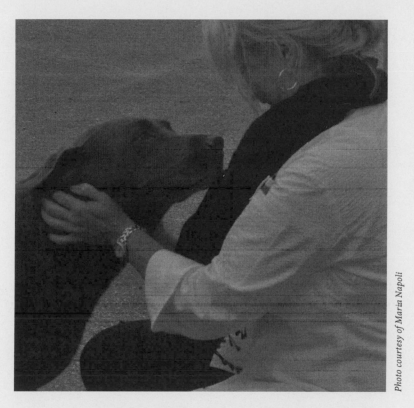

*Photo courtesy of Maria Napoli*

*When I look into the eyes of my dog*
*I smile from deep in my heart*
*See a glimpse of my soul*
*And feel unconditional love*

Maria Napoli

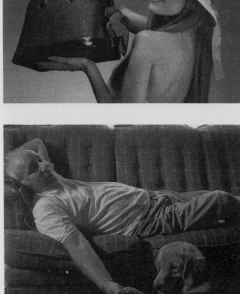

It's not a mystery that humans have a special, deeply-rooted and powerful emotional bond with their pets. Anyone who has ever had a pet knows that kindredship and love is often similar to that of a family member, because that animal has become an emotional extension of one's daily life and well-being. Those of us who have ever petted a kitten or held a puppy and smelled "puppy breath" can profess that *feel-good* emotion that often floods over us. One may notice a smile that frequently uncontrollably appears from ear-to-ear and the sparkle that lights up the eyes. It is hard to duplicate, or articulate, that certain feeling.

The American Veterinary Medical Association recognizes that "the human-animal bond is a mutually beneficial and dynamic relationship between people and animals that is influenced by behaviors that are essential to the health and well-being of both." Inclusive of this are the psychological, emotional, and physical interactions among people, animals and their collective environments.[1]

In this chapter we are going to explore beyond the anecdotal and delve into the science of this emotional and physiological bond that humans and animals share; it is this relationship that provides us benefits that are sometimes beyond immediate comprehension and are not always overt in their appearance.

## The Sensation of Touch

The initial and most common perception of a human-animal interaction is physical contact: touching, holding, and petting. This is evident in a structured environment that promotes initial interaction between people and animals, such as a petting zoo or an interactive "touch tank" at a sea life aquarium. The tactile element establishes the necessary bond that visual contact alone fails to carry.[2]

There is supportive evidence that the amygdala, the integrative center of the brain where emotion and emotional behavior live, become active beyond simple visual stimulation when touch is introduced. Emotion is activated when the sensation of touch is associated with the visual input.[3] Perhaps this is why we have this innate desire to touch something that we perceive as pleasurable such as petting a kitten or holding a puppy. This also holds true for tactile learning[4], which can be correlated with this need to touch an animal as a pleasure-seeking imprint within the brain.

The neurohormone (combination neurotransmitter and hormone) oxytocin plays an important part in the desire to hold and cuddle with an animal; often referred to as the "cuddle

drug," this short-acting chemical release in the body makes us crave physical contact and strengthens close relationships.[5] Oxytocin's role in human relationships is well-documented, but it clearly carries the same role in the human-animal dynamic.

## Emotional Engagement of the Parasympathetic Nervous System

As discussed in previous chapters but worth mentioning again, the body's physiological reaction to anxiety and stressful situations is to go into "fight or flight mode." This is the sympathetic nervous system response. Adrenalin and cortisol flood the organs and tissues, heart rate increases, the mind disengages, and the brain directs the body to go into self-preservation mode. The root of the word sympathetic is *sympathy*. Of Greek origin, the word sympathy means "to suffer."[6] Effectively, that is what your body is enduring or preparing to endure during highly anxious or stressful times.

clarissa harwell/Shutterstock.com

Opposite of this stress response is the healthy and relaxed state that occurs during engagement of the parasympathethic nervous system. Harmful chemicals released due to perceived imminent danger are replaced with endorphins, dopamine, oxytocin, etc. The prefix of the word parasympathetic is *para*. Of French origin, this prefix means "to prepare against" or "ward off."[7]

The human body cannot be in both sympathetic and parasympathetic response modes at the same time. Engagement of one disengages the other, as they stem from separate antagonistic (inhibits physiological action of another) sets of nerves.[8]

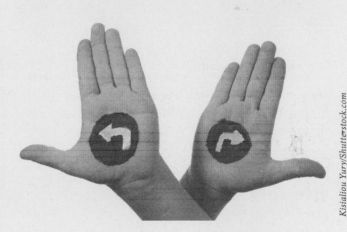

Kisialiou Yury/Shutterstock.com

Disengaging the body's sympathetic nervous system response and engaging the parasympathetic response is the fundamental component of stress management.

Interaction with an animal, be it a pet or at a petting zoo, through an animal-assisted activity or a structured therapeutic intervention, stimulates a *positive emotional state*. Animals make us smile, make us happy, and help take our minds off of things. This in itself is activation of the parasympathetic nervous system response.

Animal interaction is also mindful...*very* mindful. It is this mindfulness, this focused attention and absolute concentration on the animal that elicits a positive emotional response. (Unless, of course, you are holding a snake and you have a fear of snakes.)

# Children and Adolescents Raised With Pets

The positive feelings a child has about their immediate environment contributes to the development of their confidence and self-esteem. Such self-efficacy can be a factor for the construct of trusting relationships with others as the child grows. A positive relationship with a pet can be a foundation for the development of future healthy relationships.[9] Pet ownership and interaction with domestic animals in general not only provides the child with a connection to an element of nature, but also helps foster such developmental and cognitive skills as:[10]

Pressmaster/Shutterstock.com

- Respect for living things.
- Development of responsible behavior as a care-giver.
- Nurturing skills and empathy.
- Life lessons of birth, illness, death, and bereavement.
- Enhanced non-verbal communication.

Emotional needs can also be fulfilled as a child is often exposed to physical and psychological comfort provided by contact with the pet, as well as experiencing love, loyalty, and affection. For some children, the pet can provide a means of sharing "thoughts and secrets" in the same way a child may speak to and confide in a stuffed animal.

Prosocial behaviors, an important component of a child's development, can be enhanced through bonding and interaction with pets,[11] as there is positive and nonjudgmental affection. Studies also suggest that the introduction of a pet into the home of an autistic child can help with their socio-emotional development and prosocial behaviors.[12]

Family ownership of a pet can also improve at-home relationships because of increased time interacting and involving the animal as well as the inclusion of pet-centered activities. These increased interactions and activities promote of sense of "family harmony"[13] and connectivity between family members.

The teenage years, arguably the most challenging not only for the adolescent but also for the families themselves, are a period of identity struggle wedged in between being a child and becoming an adult. Adolescents are expected to make their own decisions, yet still have to ask permission. At a period in their lives when they may feel unloved, unaccepted, misunderstood, and at odds with the world, a pet can help provide that unconditional love, environmental stability, and emotional support.[14] Inability to clearly express emotionally-driven thoughts and coming to terms with complex and confusing feelings without an emotional outburst can be challenging at this age. Animal interaction, and even animal-assistive therapies, can help develop self-control, personal decision-making[15], and communication as their attention is redirected and focused on a specific, interactive, and engaging task.

Establishing healthy relationships and, perhaps, even mending existing ones can be promoted by the uncomplicated and unconditional love an adolescent experiences from a pet. By learning that it is "ok" to express feelings and emotions with a pet without any backlash or repercussion can provide not only an outlet for the teen but also nurture healthy relationships with friends, family, and loved ones.[16] During times when teens feel alone and depressed, a pet can provide that missing companionship.

## Adults, Young and Old, Benefit from the Human-Animal Relationship

For many adults and senior citizens, having a pet as a companion can provide not only medical benefits but also provide a level of social interaction and exercise. Pets are often viewed as a member of the family, sometimes taking the role of a child who has grown and moved out or filling the role of a deceased partner. Studies indicate that the companionship of a pet can improve the quality of life of cardiac patients by aiding in the reduction of blood pressure and assisting in recovery after a heart attack.[17] For the elderly specifically, having a pet at home has been correlated to improved overall health and self-reported well-being.[18]

*oneinchpunch/Shutterstock.com*

Emotional needs of an adult can also be fulfilled by a pet (love, loyalty and affection), as well as serve as a coping mechanism during stressful life events such as a divorce or during a time of death.[19]

Pet ownership, specifically that of a dog, can also increase a person's (both young and old) level of exercise. Many dogs require walks outdoors, which in turn provides a routine level of exercise for their owner. One study stated that the level of exercise of a dog owner "increased significantly,"[20] suggesting that canine pets have a marked impact on a sedentary lifestyle for adults of all ages. As routine exercise can be a challenge for the elderly adult, having a dog that requires outdoor activity can be exceptionally beneficial. Pets who are regularly taken outdoors often facilitate social interactions between people, leading to increased psychological health.[21] Hence, animal ownership can also improve human relationships.

## Animals as Companions…Animals as Therapy

There is a long history behind therapeutic use of animals. In the early Egyptian city of Cynopolis (City of Dogs), it was believed that if the affected area or injury were licked by a dog the individual would have a more rapid healing process or even full recovery. This practice was carried over by the Greeks.[22]

Florence Nightingale suggested that animals possessed a valuable role in adjunctive medical treatment century by writing in the late 19th: "A small pet animal is often an excellent companion for the sick, for long chronic cases especially. A pet bird in a cage is sometimes the only pleasure of an invalid confined for years to the same room."[23]

*Monkey Business Images/Shutterstock.com*

Animal-assisted interventions were present in early psychological and educational fields as well. By measuring direct physiological responses, ecologist Alan Beck and psychiatrist Aaron Katcher demonstrated a decrease in human sympathetic nervous system activity through simple interaction with a friendly dog.[24] Sigmund Freud discovered an improved outcome in his therapy sessions with children and adolescents when his dog, Jofi, was present during psychotherapy sessions.[25] John Locke in the late 1600s suggested that pet animals were conducive to childhood development and association in learning.[22]

Understanding the bond between humans and animals, and properly nurturing that bond, has opened many avenues to helping us integrate pets/animals for therapeutic, health and wellness purposes. This can be a tacit animal presence such as a house pet that provides comfort to someone at home, or more explicit and structured such as a guided interaction between a trained animal and a patient/client.

Animal-assisted interventions (animal-assisted therapies and animal-assisted activities) are a rapidly growing modality in the healthcare and educational settings. At present these interventions are considered promising complementary practices. Due to the growing alternative health movement within the established medical community, more attention is being given to these practices to identify their efficacy and validity.

Animal-assisted interventions can take the form of either Animal-Assisted Activities (AAA) or Animal-Assisted Therapies (AAT). Animal-Assisted Activities (AAA) are casual activities where an animal, its handler and an individual or group of individuals interact for comfort or recreational purposes. These activities hold minimal structure and tend not to involve patients or a formal healthcare practitioner. Animal-Assisted Therapies (AAT), conversely, are more of a structured encounter, led by a professional, involve patients/clients and are interventional to help reach specific goals in treatment.[26] Boris Levinson is widely considered the father of AAT, first demonstrating the social-behavioral benefits of animal therapy with children.[27]

Each modality relies upon, and nurtures, the human/animal bond. Dogs, cats, and horses are the most commonly used animals in Animal-Assisted Therapy. The specific type of animal utilized varies, depending on the patient's treatment plan and specific therapeutic goals to be reached.

Animal-Assisted Therapy can be employed to promote recovery and coping skills for those with health problems such as cancer, heart disease, and mental health disorders. These therapies can also significantly reduce depression, pain, anxiety and fatigue associated these disorders.[28]

Specifically, this therapeutic approach is intended to enhance physical, emotional, cognitive, and social function (American Veterinary Medical Association, 2013). Some examples are[29]:

- Improve fine motor skills.
- Increase self-esteem.
- Decrease anxiety.
- Develop social skills.
- Provide palliative care for patients undergoing chemotherapy.
- Aid long-term care facility residents.
- Assist Veterans with Post-Traumatic Stress Disorder (PTSD).
- Assist stroke victims and physical therapy patients.
- Assist mental health patients.

## ACTIVITY: YOUR FAVORITE PET OR AN ANIMAL THAT YOU HAVE HAD EXPERIENCE WITH

*"It often happens that a man is more humanely related to a cat or dog than to any human being."*

—Henry David Thoreau[30]

What was the name of your favorite pet? Or an animal you have had experience with?

_____

What kind of animal was it?

_____

List five things about this animal that made you happy:

1. _____

2. _____

3. _____

4. _____

5. _____

# Predator or Prey: Differences in the Construct of the Human-Animal Relationship

All animals (humans included) are identified as either predators or prey through evolutionary and social-behavioral characteristics. It is a wide-held belief that humans are predatory in nature based on our pre-historic ancestors; what makes this interesting, however, is that humans have demonstrated throughout history the advantages of *group living*. This demonstrates that we are, in fact, an evolved prey species.[31] According to Michael Mountain *(Why Humans are So Bad at Being Predators)*, "We are not true predators; we are, rather, a kind of empowered prey species." [31]

The human predatory background evolved when tools, which eventually spurred the development of weapons, were utilized for survival. Species of prey live in groups as protection against predators, safety in numbers, if you will. Humans are social animals; our well-being and survival dependent upon our socialization skills. This distinction of predatory versus prey behavior in humans is important in understanding how the relational dynamic between humans and animals is built.

Dogs and cats, the most recognized domesticated pets, are predatory in nature. The American Society for the Prevention of Cruelty to Animals (ASPCA) identifies the predatory nature of dogs and cats as the following:

## Dogs

Photo courtesy of Maria Napoli

- Dogs are categorized as cursorial predators. Cursorial predators chase down their prey.

- Undomesticated dogs travel in packs. Unlike prey animals that group or herd for protection against a threat, dogs will pack in order to effectively attack as a compensatory measure for their relative small size.

- Predatory aggression is different from canine aggression. Predatory aggression is non-threatening. It is non-protective. This behavior relies upon stealth to attack, whereas canine aggression is protective and alarmist.

## Cats

gilmar/Shutterstock.com

- Cats are either free-ranging (within the confines of a structured environment), feral (unsocialized), or stray (domesticated but displaced).

- Cats will explore, hunt, and scavenge for food.

- Household cats become restless and yearn for the outdoors when boredom sets in.

Domestication of dogs and cats, through training and discipline, is designed to tether their predatory nature. However, domesticated pets cannot be de-programmed from their biological predatory nature.[32] This does not mean dogs and cats are not excellent companions. Due to their predatory nature, either animal can travel and find its own food, water, and shelter; however, it is the presence of a human master that replaces the need to find their own food, water, and shelter. This is the bond that is created between us—literally that of provider-recipient. We provide not only the physiological necessities for the animal, but also the social component.

Dogs and cats demonstrate a level of reciprocity and show affection, loyalty and a protective nature of their home and provider. When that bond is violated (through abuse, neglect, or a predatory act), the animal will begin demonstrating aggressive behavior and the reciprocity of affection, loyalty, and protection becomes withdrawn. With time, that animal can develop a fear and distrust of humans.

Horses also play a strong role in understanding the human-animal relationship. Unlike domesticated house pets, horses are unique in many respects. Yet the dynamic of their relationship with humans is unmistakable and very strong.

It is, however, comparatively less popular and their value to human health and well-being is not as well-documented or demonstrated; this is due, obviously, to not only financial and space considerations, but also to accessibility and availability to the common public in addition to the lack of strong research and empirically-supportive data. The strongest testaments of the strength and value of the human-equine relationship is historically anecdotal and compartmentalized.

A horse's natural behavior and reaction to its environment are unique in this context because they are prey animals; as such their initial response to events that pose a threat or are scary to them is *flight*.[33] This is substantially different from that of a dog or cat whose initial response to similar threats or fears would be to *fight*. These are the sympathetic nervous system differences between a predatory animal and an animal of prey. There are characteristics and social-behavioral traits unique to a horse compared to the common domesticated house pet.[33]

antoriodiaz/Shutterstock.com

- Horses rely on humans, solely, for food in a domesticated environment.
- Horses are cognizant of a human's physical approach to them based on the direction of our vision. Specifically if we look at them intensely and in the eye, the horse perceives this as a predatory approach.
- Horses are keenly aware of a predatory animal and will immediately feel threatened, or at very least, uncomfortable by that presence.
- Being a 1,000-pound animal, a human's initial approach to a horse is trepidation. We are larger and more capable of physically controlling a cat or dog; not a horse. The horse can sense this trepidation and may perceive it as a threat.
- Being prey animals, horses are incredibly social and rely heavily upon social companionship, but only from a non-predatory animal.
- A horse's behavior is reflective of the human emotion it is interacting with.
- A horse senses emotions and pheromones in humans and will react accordingly.[33]
- A horse will react negatively toward a human's high energy level. Excitability and playfulness are not conducive to a horse's demeanor.[33]

What makes horses unique companions is that their reliance upon human interaction is incredibly social and is learned through their perception of and comfort level with people, unlike the domesticated house pet's reciprocity for the provision of food, water, and shelter.

The "unconditional love" that a house pet may demonstrate even when we are having the worst of days and are in emotional turmoil is not how a horse will react. The horse will sense this "uneasiness" and will shy away.[33]

When experiencing a mindful moment with an animal, one must give their intentional awareness of the present moment. Be fully in the present and practice these steps:

1. Acknowledge the moment being spent with the animal.
2. Pay full attention to the mannerisms, behaviors, and emotions shared by you and the animal.
3. Accept this moment without judgment, as the animal is not judging you nor should you judge your own feelings and emotions.
4. Choose to allow this moment to have a positive impact on you and the animal with which you are interacting.

4 Step **MAC** Guide
Mindfully
acknowledge
attention
accept
choose

## ACTIVITY: MINDFUL INTERACTION WITH ANIMALS

*"Lots of people talk to animals...Not very many listen, though... That's the problem."*

—Benjamin Hoff, The Tao of Pooh[34]

How do you feel pets demonstrate mindfulness toward their owners? List some specific examples:

_____

_____

_____

_____

How can a pet owner reciprocate that mindfulness toward their pet?

_____

_____

_____

_____

Think about the last time you were mindfully engaged with an animal that was not your pet. What drew you to interact with that animal?

_____

_____

What was your mood/state of mind?

_____

_____

How did you feel afterward?

_____

_____

# An Experiential Case Study of Equine-Assisted Activity and Therapy

## ENVISION™ Equine Assisted Therapeutic Activities & Resource Center

A wonderful demonstration of the connection between the person and the animal would be an experience on a ranch with equine-assisted therapy. The purpose of this particular therapeutic intervention is to harness the unique power of the horse to foster a calm and relaxing environment for the client. These horses respond to clients who are frightened, defensive, angry, depressed, or who demonstrate a heightened sense of anxiety and help them reach a state of physical and psychological calmness which allows them to heal and learn.

Juergen Faelchle/Shutterstock.com

A powerful observation during this experience was how these horses appeared to be so "mindfully" aware of the emotional state that people were in. The level of engagement the horse had with people was a direct reflection of the level of emotion, or lack thereof, demonstrated by that person. As an example, when participating in a very logical, emotionless conversation outside of the horse stalls, the animals were noticeably absent; however, when the conversation became a dialogue involving an emotional topic and one of personal vulnerability, the horses appeared as if they were more at-ease with the human presence at that point. As it was explained by the Life Coach and Certified Equine Specialist, the horses sensed the human emotion and no longer felt as if there was a threat from the person. As animals of prey, they are attuned to an anxious, disconnected presence and may perceive that more of a threat than something that is welcomed.[35]

These horses would also demonstrate anxiety if the client they were working with was anxious. As the client was coached into a relaxed state and felt more comfortable being around the horse, the horse moved closer to the client and would actually begin nuzzling them. Such an incredible demonstration of the mindful connectivity between human and animal. The partnership observed between the horse and human relied heavily upon a relaxed, emotional connectivity so that the partnership could be built.

Unlike petting a dog or holding a cat, riding a horse implies a certain level of potential danger. There appeared to be a level of trust and vulnerability that had to be shared with the animal to put both the horse and rider at ease and foster that partnership.

## ACTIVITY: ADOPTING A PET

*"Whoever declared that love at first sight doesn't exist has never witnessed the purity of a puppy or looked deep into a puppy's eyes. If they did, their lives would change considerably."*

—Elizabeth Parker, Paw Prints in the Sand[36]

This activity will require you to visit a pet adoption event or center of some sort. While at this event or center please limit yourself to ten minutes of engagement with the animal. This is crucial because the purpose of this activity is to reach into your emotional responses, not your logical/cognitive analysis. When responding to the following questions, document your initial thoughts…the first things that come to your mind…write them down. Use very few words. Do not script or analyze your words. Pure emotional responses. Don't respond with what you think. Respond with what you FEEL.

Find a puppy. If you can hold this puppy, do. If not, then look into its eyes.

What do you feel?

_____

_____

What is the puppy feeling?

_____

_____

After your ten minutes has passed, leave the event or center.

Now…how do you feel?

_____

_____

## Why Animals and Not People?

The human-animal relationship holds, at its cornerstone, engagement at a truly *mindful* level. This would include active mindfulness on behalf of the person and innate mindfulness on behalf of the animal. There is a mutually reciprocative, mindful engagement between humans and animals. A person seeks companionship, love, and satisfaction in caring for an animal. In exchange, the animal bonds with the person, satisfies that need for love and companionship, and relies upon the person to be taken care of. Neither human nor animal judge each other and they act upon each other's moods, mannerisms, and perceived situational needs. This is a level of intentional attention, emotional engagement, and non-verbal awareness that provides the mindfulness of their relationship.

*Daxiao Productions/Shutterstock.com*

It is not being suggested that animals take the place of other people as a means to satisfy our social-behavioral construct or our need for bonding. Not at all. What is being suggested is that animals can fill voids, mental or social, that different people may have due to varying circumstances. Perhaps these are needs that are unable to be filled by another person. These voids can often be the need to self-reflect and respond to individual stressors in a very private, personal fashion or perhaps in another fashion that is unavailable for certain reasons.

Mindful engagement…building that human/animal bond…requires a level of vulnerability; a level of emotional vulnerability that often is difficult to share with another person. Animals do not judge people. People judge people. The human-animal dynamic carries within itself a strong level of nonjudgmental interaction. Animals provide a level of unconditional love, respect, and loyalty with very little required of their human counterpart. What animals do require is our mindful attention to the very basic of human and animal needs and instincts.

## References

1. American Veterinary Medical Association. Retrieved from http://avma.org/

2. Anderson, D., Piscitelli, B., Weier, K., Everett, M., & Tayler, C. (2002), Children's museum experiences: Identifying powerful mediators of learning. *Curator: The Museum Journal, 45*: 213–231. doi: 10.1111/j.2151-6952.2002.tb00057

3. Gordon, I., Voos, A. C., Bennett, R. H., Bolling, D. Z., Pelphrey, K. A., & Kaiser, M. D. (2013), Brain mechanisms for processing affective touch. *Hum. Brain Mapp., 34:* 914–922. doi: 10.1002/hbm.21480.

4. Harris, J. A., Harris, I. M., & Diamond, M. E. (2001). The topography of tactile learning in humans. *The Journal of Neuroscience, 21*(3): 1056–1061.

5. De Dreu, C. K., Greer, L. L., Van Kleef, G. A., Shalvi, S., & Handgraaf, M. J. (2011). Oxytocin promotes human ethnocentrism. *Proceedings of the National Academy of Sciences, 108*(4): 1262–1266.

6.  sympathy. (n.d.). *Dictionary.com Unabridged*. Retrieved from  http://dictionary.reference.com/browse/sympathy

7.  para. (n.d.). *Dictionary.com Unabridged*. Retrieved from http://dictionary.reference.com/browse/para

8.  autonomic nervous system. (2015). In *Encyclopædia Britannica*. Retrieved from http://www.britannica.com/EBchecked/topic/45079/autonomic-nervous-system

9.  Pets and children, American academy of child and adolescent psychiatry. (2013, May). *Facts for Families*, No. 75.

10. Pruitt, D. (1998). *Your child: What every parent needs to know about childhood development from birth to preadolescence.* New York: Harper Collins.

11. Endenburg, N., & Baarda, B. (1996). The role of pets in enhancing human well-being: Effects on child development. In: I. Robinson I (Ed.), *The Waltham book of human-animal interactions: Benefits and responsibilities of pet ownership* (pp.7–17). Oxford, UK: Elsevier.  Oxford, UK.

12. Grandgeorge, M., Tordjman, S., Lazartigues, A., Lemonnier, E., Deleau, M., & Hausberger, M. (2012). Does pet arrival trigger prosocial behaviors in individuals with autism? *PloS one, 7*(8), e41739.

13. The Royal Children's Hospital Melbourne. (2015, Feb. 3). *Dogs and Kids: Benefits of Pets.* Retrieved at http://www.rch.org.au/dogsandkids/benefits/

14. Alicie, Suzanne. (2010, March). The benefits of pets for teenagers. *Canidae*. Retrieved at http://www.canidae.com/blog/2010/03/benefits-of-pets-for-teenagers.html

15. What is equine-assisted psychotherapy? (2015). *CRC Health Group.* 2015.

16. Mallon, G. P. (1994, April). Some of our best therapists are dogs. In *Child and Youth Care Forum*. Vol. 23, No. 2: 89–101. Kluwer Academic Publishers-Human Sciences Press.

17. Health enhancement and companion animal ownership. (1996, May). *Annual Review of Public Health,* Vol. 17: 247-257. DOI: 10.1146/annurev.pu.17.050196.001335

18. Beck, A.M., Meyers, N.M. (1996). Health enhancement and companion animal ownership. *Annual Review of Public Health 17*:247–257. doi: 10.1146/annurev.publhealth.17.1.247

19. Sable, P. (1995). Pets, attachment, and well-being across the life cycle. *Social work, 40*(3): 334–341.

20. Serpell, J. (1991). Beneficial effects of pet ownership on some aspects of human health and behaviour. *Journal of the Royal Society of Medicine, 84*(12), 717–720.

21. Wells, D. L. (2004). The facilitation of social interactions by domestic dogs. *Anthrozoos: A Multidisciplinary Journal of The Interactions of People & Animals, 17*(4), 340–352.

22. Fine, A. H. (Ed.). (2010). *Handbook on animal-assisted therapy: Theoretical foundations and guidelines for practice.* San Diego, CA: Academic Press.

23. Nightingale, F. (1969.) Notes on nursing: What it is, and what it is not. New York: Dover, 103.

24. Beck, A.M., & Katcher, A. H. (1996). *Between pets and people: The importance of animal companionship.* West Lafayette, IN: Purdue University Press.

25. Coren, S., & Bartlet, A. (2002). *The pawprints of history: Dogs and the course of human events.* New York: Free Press

26. Animal-Assisted Activities/Therapy 101. (2012). *Pet Partners.* Retrieved http://www.petpartners.org/AAA-Tinformation

27. Levinson, B. M. (1962). The dog as a" co-therapist." *Mental Hygiene. New York.*

28. DeCourcey, M., et al. (2010). Animal-assisted therapy: Evaluation and implementation of a complementary therapy to improve the psychological and physiological health of critically ill patients. *Dimensions of Critical Care Nursing. 2010;29:211.*

29. Cole, K. M., Gawlinski, A., Steers, N., & Kotlerman, J. (2007, November). Animal-assisted therapy in patients hospitalized with heart failure. *American Journal of Critical Care, 16(6),* 575–585.

30. Thoreau, H. D. (1906). *The Writings of Henry David Thoreau: The Maine Woods.* Boston: Houghton Mifflin.

31. Hart, D., Sussman, R. W. (2005) *Man the hunted: Primates, predators, and human evolution.* New York: Westview.

32. Virtual Pet Behavorist. (2015, Jan. 4). *ASPCA.* Retrieved at http://www.aspca.org/pet-care?ref=driverlayer.com/web

33. Evans, P. (2010). *Equine behavior: Prey vs. predator, horse vs. human.* Logan, UT: Utah State University.

34. Hoff, B. (1982). *The tao of Pooh* (Vol. 1). New York: EP Dutton.

35. Péwé, L. (2015, Sep-Nov). In-person interviews.

36. Parker, E. (2015, Feb. 23). Elizabeth Parker-Author of Thrillers and Books about Dogs-Home. Retrieved at http://topfamousquotes.com/quotes/whoever-declared-that-love-at-first-sight-doesnt-exist-has-148458/

## CHAPTER 7 QUESTIONS

1.  What is the difference between a predatory and a prey animal?

2.  What are some of the benefits of Animal Assisted Therapy to a patient/client?

3.  What is the definition of an Animal Assisted Activity?

4. In reference to the human-animal relationship, how does a horse differ from a house pet?

5. Explain your understanding of the difference between the sympathetic and parasympathetic-nervous systems?

6. Which do animals respond to: emotion or logic?

# MINDFUL AWARENESS REFLECTION JOURNAL

Choose one mindful experience as you begin your reflection.

### Empathically Acknowledge

Describe your experience.

_____

_____

_____

### Intentional Attention

Describe what you noticed.

| |
|---|
| Breath |
| Body |
| Emotions |
| Thoughts |
| Senses |

### Accept Without Judgment

Describe judgment; acceptance.

_____

_____

_____

### Willingly Choose

Choose to purposely respond to your experience.

_____

_____

_____

### Mindful Mac Meditation

Describe your meditation experiences. What did you learn from your meditation experience?

_____

_____

_____

# Mindful Daily Journal

**TODAY'S Insight WOW!**

_____

_____

_____

_____

_____

_____

_____

_____

_____

_____

_____

_____

_____

_____

_____

_____

_____

_____

_____

_____

_____

*Tips for Wellbeing*

- Have Hope
- Accept Yourself
- Exercise
- Practice Mindfulness
- Express Gratitude
- Master Your Environment
- Find Purpose
- Stay Connected
- Be an Optimist

_____

_____

_____

_____

Date: _____ Make Today Count!

# CHAPTER 8

# Harmony Across the Lifespan: The Benefits of Music Throughout Our Lives

**Charles Tyler and Eric Shetzen**

*Photo courtesy of Maria Napoli*

*There is music everywhere*

*Birds singing*

*Wind blowing*

*Leaves rustling*

*Close your eyes and listen to the music*

*In concert,*

*In your mind*

*In your heart*

*Today and Everyday*

Maria Napoli

*"Without music, life would be a mistake."*

—Friedrich Nietzsche[1]

What is your favorite song? Can you remember the first time you heard it? What is it about that song that makes it so special? Whether it be a classical symphony or a chart-topping hit, chances are listening to or playing music makes you feel good. What exactly is it about music that makes us experience feelings of joy, nostalgia, excitement, or relaxation? Only recently has scientific research begun to delve into the positive effects that music has on our brain and bodies.

There are different ways in which we all experience music throughout our lives. There are numerous positive effects that occur when one is directly involved in music through playing or singing or indirectly involved through listening. In young children, music plays a huge role in their development and their ability to learn. Music can also help busy adults relax and reduce their levels of stress. Later in life, music has the ability to assist people with combating certain illnesses, such as Alzheimer's, as well as easing pain and providing a sense of nostalgia to older adults. In this chapter, you will learn about the benefits music provides across the lifespan and how one can achieve a higher quality of life through musical enjoyment.

Tepikina Nastya/Shutterstock.com

The benefits that come along with experiencing music can be observed in the earliest stages of life. It has been shown that babies exposed to music while still in the womb have been able to recognize and prefer music that they heard prenatally a year later[2]. This fact can be supported by the child's preference for its mother's voice, as this is the sound that it had experienced more than any other before coming into the world. It must be noted that learning begins for the fetus once necessary brain development has taken place (several months before birth), and listening to music has been shown to stimulate the brain's cognitive language development. Current research has shown that "music and language are so intertwined that an awareness of music is critical to a baby's language development.… As children grow, music fosters communication skills. Our sense of song helps us learn to talk, read, and even make friends."[3] In addition, music has been shown to alleviate stress and can help a mother keep her baby healthy. Studies reveal that "when a pregnant woman is chronically stressed or experiences extreme stress, the baby may be exposed to unhealthy levels of stress hormones, which can impact the baby's brain development."[4] High levels of stress in mothers have been connected to premature births as well as lower IQ in children.

The positive effects music provides are not limited to infants and the very young. Children's skill sets are enhanced by learning music during the elementary education level (ages 7–13) and these benefits have been shown to encompass a wide variety of areas including but not limited to numeracy, creativity, motor coordination, and improved personal and social development. Students' success in music improves confidence and self-esteem, as well as increases motivation for study in other subject areas.[5] Music education organizations such as *El Sistema* in Venezuela, which seeks to empower impoverished youth through music education, are proving to the world that music has the capability of providing stability and opportunity. In addition to musical ability, students of such a program as *El Sistema*, many of whom are often faced with enormous socio-economic challenges, acquire discipline, teamwork skills, self-confidence, a sense of accomplishment, and many other essential components for a healthy, balanced life. Much research on music education has shown that "youth music participation is associated with higher matriculation rates (Aschaffenburg and Maas, 1997), higher rates of acceptance into medical schools (Thomas, 1994), lower rates of current and lifetime alcohol, tobacco, or drug abuse (Texas Commission on Drug and Alcohol Abuse, 1999), and lower rates of disruptive classroom behaviors (National Center for Educational Statistics, 1997)."[6]

*Tomacco/Shutterstock.com*

## ACTIVITY: THE MOZART EFFECT

Listen to a piece of music by Mozart either while performing another task such as reading, studying, cooking, etc. How did the music impact your work?

_____

_____

_____

_____

How did the music make you feel while you were performing the activity?

_____

_____

_____

Did you notice any changes in your performance?

_____

_____

_____

_____

Adults who embrace music in their lives are deeply affected every day in numerous ways. Whether one turns on a particular song while taking care of day-to-day tasks or attends a once in a lifetime concert, there is a lasting effect. Listening to music has been shown to reduce stress and promote relaxation. One example of this effect can be found in observing drivers who listen to music while driving in congested areas. When stopped in seemingly endless traffic, drivers can experience frustration and symptoms of road rage. The added stress of having to be on time for an important engagement or appointment can often make the driving experience unbearable, but playing a favorite song or music from a particular artist chosen by the listener has been shown to help alleviate some of these symptoms. Listening to music has been proven to lower stress levels in areas of extremely high congestion.[7] In addition to listening to recorded music, attending concerts is a favorite past-time that allows listeners to celebrate life and experience joy. There are many benefits to attending a live music-performance

Annette Shaff/Shutterstock.com

that cannot be replicated by listening to a recording. Whether it be a hard rock concert in an arena, a classical performance in a symphony hall, or a jazz combo in a smoky cafe, the energy and excitement of live music often creates a memorable experience via the exchange of emotion from the performers to the audience. Live performance also provides the opportunity for the audience to take part in the performance itself, whether it be by clapping, dancing, or even singing along. Attending concerts is a proven way to help improve one's mood and can boost spirits for many days afterwards.

Rido/Shutterstock.com

There are many different ways in which music has been shown to help improve the quality of life for older adults. Musical memory is stored in our minds differently than other aspects of our cognitive memories. This would help explain how someone suffering from Alzheimer's can remember the words to a song from their youth yet would not be able to say what they did earlier that day. (This can also go along with how children's songs are often dedicated to the memory of useful information such as the countries of the world, the states, or the alphabet). Music therapy, the use of musical interventions in a clinical setting to accomplish individualized goals within a therapeutic relationship by a credentialed professional who has completed an approved music therapy program, has recently come to the forefront of the medical research field. There has been a great deal of research exploring the effects of music therapy on the depression and anxiety of Alzheimer's patients and the results have been astounding. "Music therapy modifies the components of the disease through sensory, cognitive, affective, and behavioral effects. Receptive music therapy encourages cognitive stimulation, allowing patients to recall autobiographical memories and images…. Music therapy, a method which is easy to apply, contributes to the treatment of anxiety disorders and depressive syndrome in patients suffering from Alzheimer's disease."[8] In addition, music has been shown to help aid in the recovery of patients after surgery. Use of music therapy with post-operative patients has "demonstrated effectiveness in reducing pain, decreasing anxiety, and increasing relaxation. In addition, music has been used as a process to distract persons from unpleasant sensations and empower them with the ability to heal from within."[9] Also, it has been shown that music therapy has been used with encouraging results as an end-of-life care regimen for hospice patients. Possible benefits of music-therapy as a part of palliative treatment include reduction of anxiety, decrease of discomfort, increase in spiritual well-being, and higher quality-of-life.[10]

*"After silence, that which comes nearest to expressing the inexpressible is music."*

—Aldous Huxley[11]

## ACTIVITY: MEMORY AND MUSIC

Try to think of a song or piece of music that holds a special meaning for you. This music could be from a particular time of your life or reminiscent of a specific event. It could also represent a more general feeling but it should be something that has personal significance. Maybe it brings back warm and fond memories, or perhaps painful ones. Have the song ready to play and below we will try to figure out what it is about this song or piece of music that brings back a certain flood of emotion. Through this activity we will gain a deeper understanding and appreciation for how music can influence our lives in profound ways.

Before listening, think about what the song means to you.

Describe.

_____

_____

_____

_____

Play the song.

Write down your reaction to the song. What emotions did you experience? What was it about hearing the song that made it easier to articulate certain feelings?

_____

_____

_____

_____

Describe what images came to mind. Did specific images come to mind before hearing the song, or did they only emerge after listening?

_____

_____

_____

_____

How can you apply what you learned in this activity to benefit your everyday life?

_____

_____

_____

_____

*"One ought, every day at least, to hear a little song, read a good poem, see a fine picture, and, if it were possible, to speak a few reasonable words."*

—Johann Wolfgang von Goethe[12]

Finding music that truly speaks to someone is a personal journey. How often have we been cornered in our habitual musical circles and then suddenly been blown away by something completely different and new? We can never assume exactly what type of music will resonate with us in a profound way

without doing some degree of exploring and leaving our comfort zone. Every one of us is different, and by that same token will have different preferences regarding how different types of music make us feel. One of the most interesting things about music is its varying effect on mood and how people can interpret the same music in completely different ways. For example, some of us, when we want to relax, listen to classical music or smooth jazz, others listen to heavy metal or punk rock. Musical tastes are extremely personal and often difficult to define, yet at the same time they are malleable and always changing throughout our lives.

## ACTIVITY: MUSICAL DISCOVERY

One of the easiest ways to explore the endless variety of music is by going on YouTube. This site is an invaluable resource for broadening one's horizons in addition to discovering particular performances and recordings. Before heading out and finding a particular performance, go on YouTube and explore the literally endless varieties of music.

Here are a few suggestions to get your wheels turning and your ears listening (these are all merely starting points for your search; see where they take you!):

1. African Drumming
2. Guillaume de Machaut: *La Messe de Nostre Dame, Kyrie*
3. Mahler: *Symphony No. 5 - Adagietto*
4. Charles Mingus: *Goodbye Pork Pie Hat*
5. Daft Punk: *One More Time*
6. Arvo Pärt: *Spiegel im Spiegel*
7. João Gilberto: *Desafinado*
8. Of Montreal: *City Bird*

Write down some of your discoveries that surprised you. Where did your search take you?

_____

_____

_____

_____

There are many ways to find and discover new types of music, but usually the most meaningful way is to experience the music live. Keep in mind that live music does not need to be experienced in a formal concert hall or stadium setting. It could be someone playing an instrument in the park, singing in a cafe, or at a concert at a nearby college. Remember that music is all around us, and often all you need to do to find it is listen. Oftentimes one can be intimidated by venturing out in search of something new, but having a strategy of how to take in unfamiliar music will help one define what they are experiencing. The activity below will help you through the process of deciphering new music.

## ACTIVITY: ENGAGE YOUR EARS!

Find and attend a concert or performance of live music that is outside of your usual listening prefer- ence, preferably a genre that you have never seen or heard before. This can be a classical symphony performance, a jazz combo, a rock show, a traditional world music performance, or any other type of live performance. Record your response to the music. What emotions did you experience? Were there any aspects of the performance that were memorable, or, perhaps, forgettable? If you had to visualize or draw the imagery that came to mind how would you describe what you saw? Be in the moment as you listen and afterwards try to respond to the following prompts.

What are the images that come to mind?

_____

_____

_____

_____

What emotions are you aware of?

_____

_____

_____

_____

How would you put into words and describe what you heard to someone who is not there hearing the music?

_____

_____

_____

_____

Is there a deeper meaning in the music?

_____

_____

_____

What about the text? How does knowing the text add to your understanding? Often times one listens to songs without really giving a close look at the lyrics or text.

_____

_____

_____

*"Those who have made music themselves understand better, and those who understand hear better. And we shall never have a world in which music is genuinely understood, appreciated, reverenced, and loved until listeners become active again—active not only in performance, but in making definite efforts to participate intelligently and receptively in all they hear."*

—Igor Stravinsky[13]

Whether you realized it or not, the activities you participated in earlier in this chapter have helped you define and hone your active listening skills. Active listening can be thought of as a way to be involved in the musical process while listening whether it involves imagining certain emotions or imagery, or acquiring a deeper meaning of the music itself. Anytime you are dedicating 100% of your attention and focus to listening to music you are actively listening. This is opposed to passive listening, which occurs when you hear music playing in the background (e.g., in a store or in an elevator). Learning to be an active listener will not only help you better understand music, but will improve your ability to retain information as well as increase your levels of creativity and motivation. It is also acknowledged that critical thinking skills are enhanced via the brain's use of analysis and synthesis of information while actively listening to music because "these processes support higher-order thinking and promote the experience of the arts as expressions of critical thought."[14]

In addition to active listening, there are many other ways one can participate in music including, but not limited to, singing, playing, and dancing. Singing is one of the purest forms of human expression; whether alone in the shower, with friends at a karaoke bar, or even in more formal settings such as in a church choir or other performing ensemble, singing allows the voice to convey emotions that cannot be communicated through language alone.

Dancing is one of the most ancient and primal modes of expression, which dates back to the earliest known civilizations. Dance focuses on using the body to physically react and respond to music. Playing a musical instrument is one of our oldest pastimes. From the most simple rhythmic instruments to the extremely complex electronic instruments of today, musical instruments have assisted us in producing and performing our music for thousands of years.

## ACTIVITY: GET INVOLVED!

You have learned about the various ways one can participate in music, and now it is time to get involved!

Choose one method of participating in music (singing, dancing, or playing an instrument).

Find an outlet/location in which to perform, either solo or with others. This does not have to be a formal concert; it can be as simple as singing karaoke, taking a piano lesson, or attending a salsa class.

Perform and experiment in your chosen mode of musical expression.

Describe your experience. How did it make you feel? What did you enjoy/not enjoy about the experience?

_____

_____

_____

_____

_____

*Sheftsoff Stock Photo/Shutterstock.com*

In this chapter you have learned about the effects of music throughout various stages and aspects of our lives. The beneficial effects of exposure to music begin before we are born and continue to nurture us during our various stages of development until the ends of our lives. Music has been a central part of the human experience throughout history and embracing the diversity of music can reveal surprising discoveries and lead to deeper understanding within one's own life. Music has the ability to help us learn, help us feel, help us relax, and help us lead more fulfilling lives.

# References

1. Nietzsche, F. (2009 ed.) In *The twilight of the idols and the anti-Christ*. Penguin Classics. London: Penguin Books.

2. Levitin, D.J. (2006). *This is your brain on music: The science of a human obsession*. New York, NY: Dutton, 261.

3. Schiller, P. (2010). Early brain development research review and update. *Brain Development Nov/Dec, 26–30*.

4.  Johnson, K. (2007). The effects of maternal stress and anxiety during pregnancy. *Maternal Substance Abuse and Child Development Project*, Emory University, pp. 1–3.

5.  Hallam, S. (2010). The power of music: Its impact on the intellectual, social and personal development of children and young people. *International Journal of Music Education*, p. 17.

6.  Southgate, D. E., & Roscigno, V. J. (2009). The Impact of Music on Childhood and Adolescent Achievement. *Social Science Quarterly, Vol. 90, No. 1*, pp. 4–21.

7.  Wiesenthal, D. L., Hennessy, D. A & Totten, B. (2006). The influence of music on driver stress. *Journal of Applied Social Psychology, Vol. 30, Issue 8*, pp. 1709–19. (p. 1716).

8.  Guétin, S., Portet, F., & Picot, M-C. (2009). Effect of music therapy on anxiety and depression in patients with Alzheimer's type dementia: Randomised, controlled study. *Dementia and Geriatric Cognitive Disorders*, pp. 36–46 (p. 45).

9.  McCaffrey, R. and Locsin, R.C.. (2002). Music listening as a nursing intervention: A symphony of practice. *Holistic Nursing Practice, Vol. 16, Issue 3*, pp. 70–77.

10. Hilliard, R. E. (2005). Music therapy in hospice and palliative care: A review of the empirical data. *Evidence-Based Complementary and Alternative Medicine, Vol. 2(2)*, pp. 173–178.

11. Brooke, J. (2002). *Don't let death ruin your life: A practical guide to reclaiming happiness after the death of a loved one*. New York, Penguin Publishing, p. 243.

12. Goethe, J. W. von. (1917, 2001). *Wilhelm Meister's Apprenticeship*. Vol. XIV. Harvard Classics Shelf of Fiction. New York: P.F. Collier & Son, 1917; Bartleby.com, 2001. www.bartleby.com/314/

13. Stravinsky, I. (1934, August). As I see myself: Stravinsky on his life as a composer. *Gramophone Magazine, August 1934*.

14. Johnson, Daniel C. (2004). Music listening and critical thinking: Teaching using a constructivist paradigm. *International Journal of the Humanities, Vol. 2, Issue 2*, pp. 1161–1169 (p. 1166).

# MINDFUL AWARENESS REFLECTION JOURNAL

4 Step MAC Guide

Choose one mindful experience as you begin your reflection.

## Empathically Acknowledge

Describe your experience.

_____

_____

_____

## Intentional Attention

Describe what you noticed.

| Breath |  |
|--------|--|
| Body |  |
| Emotions |  |
| Thoughts |  |
| Senses |  |

## Accept Without Judgment

Describe judgment; acceptance.

_____

_____

_____

## Willingly Choose

Choose to purposely respond to your experience.

_____

_____

_____

## Mindful Mac Meditation

Describe your meditation experiences. What did you learn from your meditation experience?

_____

_____

_____

# Mindful Daily Journal

TODAY'S insight WOW!

_____
_____
_____
_____
_____
_____
_____
_____
_____
_____
_____
_____
_____
_____
_____
_____
_____
_____
_____
_____
_____

*Tips for Wellbeing*

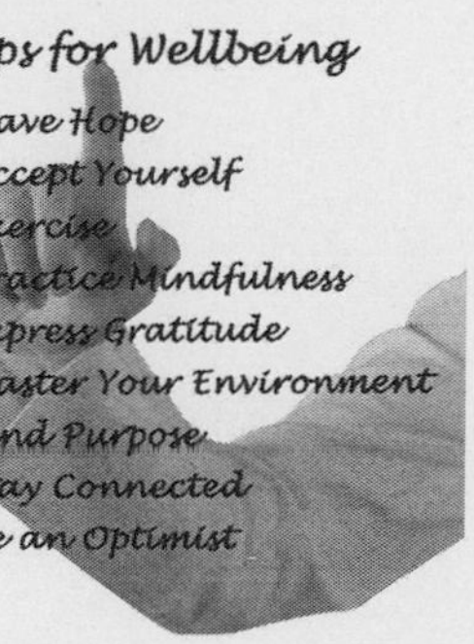

- Have Hope
- Accept Yourself
- Exercise
- Practice Mindfulness
- Express Gratitude
- Master Your Environment
- Find Purpose
- Stay Connected
- Be an Optimist

_____
_____
_____
_____

Date: _____  Make Today Count!

# The Artist Within Across the Lifespan

**Olga Idriss Davis**

*Photo courtesy of Maria Napoli*

*Imagination is the light to creativity*

*We all possess it*

*Cultivate*

*Share*

*Transform yourself*

Maria Napoli

189

*The artist comes to the stage of life*
*Expecting nothing but giving all*
*With each word, sound, gesture, colorful expression*
*A life is touched and the world is renewed*
*Don't be afraid to reach*
*Reaching is our goal*
*Yes, the goal of life is to reach our greatest potential*
*As creative beings across the span of a lifetime.*[1]

—Olga Idriss Davis

In this book, you have been introduced to many concepts about whole person health. Now, we are going to discuss your identity as an artist, what the artist within means, and how to develop your unique artistry—being mindful of creativity across your lifetime.

*Finding the artist within means to find truth within yourself. An artist is a truth-seeker.*[2]

Julian G. Davis, Jazz Harmonicist

# Setting the Stage: The Lifespan

Human communication theory suggests that communication is a central meaning to human experience.[3] Humans communicate by the creative dimensions of the self. That means, we learn about the world through our five senses—taste, touch, smell, hearing, and sight. We become aware of our world, try to negotiate its meaning with others, and create new systems of knowing to help build community and enhance self-identity. The ways in which we communicate our knowledge of the world to ourselves are part of the caring process. To engage in artistry as an artist, or a truth seeker, wisdom bearer, and one who dares to reach one's highest potential, begins the caring-healing practices and process of mindfulness. The lifespan approach to locating the artist within, points to the importance of locating creativity.

Erik Erikson characterized the lifespan theory as a struggle between basic trust and mistrust.[4] Central to Erikson's theory of the lifespan is a challenge to the ego, a threat, but also an opportunity to grow and to

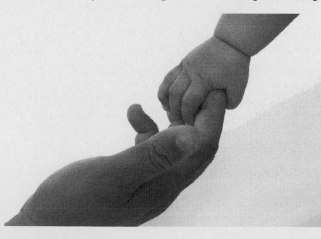
infocus/Shutterstock.com

improve.[5] In his psychosocial developmental scheme, there are eight stages of development that occur throughout the lifespan: trust versus mistrust; autonomy versus shame and doubt; initiative versus guilt; industry versus inferiority; identity versus role confusions; intimacy versus isolation; generativity versus stagnation; ego integrity versus despair. In the stages which parallel preschool, school age, and adolescence, the behavior is reflected in learning how children assert control and power over the environment, how to cope and negotiate social and academic demands;

and how to develop a sense of self and personal identity while navigating the social relationships of their world. In adulthood, whether it be the stages of young adulthood, middle adulthood, or maturity, adults are challenged to seek outcomes that form intimate, loving relationships with other people; create and nurture things that will outlast us and help us in feeling useful and accomplished; and to be able to reflect on our life with a sense of fulfillment and wisdom to impart to the next generation.

As in life, there is dynamic energy within each of the stages. The outcomes that arise from each stage demonstrate basic conflict when searching for the truth within. These tensions arise when we doubt ourselves and are unsure of our skills and assets. We become negligent of the idea to release the dynamism that propels us forward despite the small voice of doubt lingering inside. We try to achieve balance, yet we vacillate between the desires of life and the needs of daily living, creating a tension that oftentimes serves as a catalyst for dis-ease in our bodies—high blood pressure, anxiety, heart disease, diabetes, panic attacks, and on and on.

Naypong/Shutterstock.com

I contend we are seeking the creative artist that links us to the truth within. In the lifespan stages from infancy to old age, the artist within seeks to find genius, authenticity, ingenuity, and a belief system from which to thrive. From the incipience of birth, the infant creates an identity close to its mother, but begins the creative process by learning how to navigate her/his surroundings. If you've ever watched a baby, you will see how she listens attentively to every sound, how he watches every movement, how she is aroused by familiar voices, and slowly but surely, learns to perform in their environments—learning to negotiate the need for food, sustenance, comfort, touch, involvement with other human beings, and love. Most importantly on the lifespan of infancy to adulthood is the creative power of love, of giving back to others, and of evolving the self during the life course.[6]

## Centering the Body

*Centering* means to find yourself at the center of energy, of light, and of space—signifying an understanding of your place and meaning in the world. Centering means to locate your own story within the ordinariness of daily life as a means of creatively surviving the vicissitudes of life.[7] Centering the body means to locate the meaning of self through the body; to sense, to feel, and to act become a way of seeing the world through body knowledge, or self-centering. To believe there is a reason for your existence and that you are meant to be here—right here, right now, is very empowering. The recognition of this is the assuredness that creativity and identity will bond in the intertextuality of self and being. For each individual, the journey of centering ourselves is different. However, when we challenge or dare to explore beyond our boundaries of constraints and fears of failing, we are in direct parallel to the artist within—creativity is boundless, but must be unlocked through centering the body.

THE BODY ACHIEVES WHAT THE MIND BELIEVES

Naypong/Shutterstock.com

The corporeal body is foundational to the performance of the artist. The body is grounded in the knowledge of the lived experience, and thus, its memories of past and present are the essence of that which is within. The body informs through kinesthetic memory, DNA recall, and body knowledge. The body's authenticity is a bridge connecting the past to the present; it reveals truth to build on for the future.[8] Its passion and growth are located in the very sinews and arteries, vessels and bloodlines of the pulsating heartbeats, the ebbs-and-flows of blood pressure and balance. So then, when we talk about the body as a system of creativity, it is here that the energy emanates, dissipates, and transforms in the process of becoming.

## ACTIVITY: CENTER YOUR BODY AND CLEAR YOUR MIND THROUGH BREATHING

Lie on the floor in a supine position. Close your eyes. Turn your palms upward. Let your body sink deeper and deeper into the floor. Breathe from the diaphragm on counts of three: Inhale 1, 2, 3—Exhale 1, 2, 3. Think of nothing but the inhale-exhale process of breathing. Repeat for five minutes (practice the three part breath on your Mindful MAC Reflections CD).

# An Artistic Identity

The traditional definition and concept of an artist is a person possessing unusual creativity in any field. When we think of conveying an identity as an artist, we think that means someone with great potential, or someone who has been born with extreme talent, skills, and abilities. However, to be mindful of the artist within "dares" us to see the world through the creativity within ourselves. While we may not have the special talents of unusual creativity or extraordinary ability, each individual has a degree of creative capacity if she or he dares to see it, acknowledge it, develop it, and embrace the capacity for change, growth, and creativity.[9]

whiteisthecolor/Shutterstock.com

I want you to embrace a new definition of artistic identity. I want you to think of what it means to be an artist in three ways: (1) an artist is a truth-seeker; (2) an artist is a wisdom-bearer; and, (3) an artist is not afraid to reach. The goal of the artist is found in the symbolic and literal act of *reaching*.

## Who Is an Artist?

Creative talent means greater sensitivity to sensory stimulation, unusual capacity for awareness of relations between various stimuli, predisposition to an empathy of wider range and deeper vibration than usual, and sensorimotor equipment for building up projective motor discharges for expressive functions. P. Greenacre says, "…genius is a gift of the gods, and is already laid down at birth."[10] The artistic product is a love gift to the world. There is no intrinsic connection between talent and neurosis. Direction of development of genius or talent is largely determined by identifications. Creative activity is the life source to counteract fear, provide a sense of positive self-confidence, and develop a curiosity for wonderment.[11]

During my travels to Machu Picchu, the ancient city of the Incas in the Andes Mountains of Peru, I reflected on the artistry of a people and the artist within. What struck me most in this lost city 13,000 feet above sea level, was the notion that regardless of the artistic product generated by the geniuses of architecture, space, astronomy, and of aesthetics, there was an energy which sought truth. In Incan civilization, seeking truth illuminated the voice of a people reflected in their designed, engineered, symbolic craftsmanship of art to honor its role of creating and maintaining community.

R. Gino Santa Maria/Shutterstock.com

What I began to realize at Machu Picchu was that artists have tapped into the creative energy that is all around us in the universe as a means of locating truth. An artist is a creative individual who dares to search within to reveal the self and to seek truth.

## A Truth-Seeker

In finding the truth about ourselves and thus unlocking the potential of creativity and artistry within, we offer a couple of activities that can begin the process of truth-seeking.

### ACTIVITY: YOUR NAME

Locate the meaning of your name. When you have found the meaning of your name, draw a picture as best you can of your visualization of that meaning. Then, go to the garden nearest you, and bury in the soil the picture you have drawn. Upon reflection ask yourself, "What is my truth? Who am I right now—today? What have I buried? What characteristics do I need to work on?" Do you agree or disagree with the meaning of your name? Does your name correspond with your identity as you currently see yourself?

_____

_____

_____

## ACTIVITY: TRUTH JAR

Select a box, a jar, a Tupperware dish, a vase, some sort of container, and name it, "My Truth Jar." In this jar, you are to place all of your affirmations. An affirmation is a strong, positive statement that something is already so.[12] Some examples of affirmations taken from the text, *The Artist's Way*[13], include: "As I create and listen, I will be led." "My creativity always leads me to truth and to love." "I am willing to learn to let myself create." "I am willing to use my creative talents." Try these affirmations and see if you can create others on your own.

# A Wisdom-Bearer

*"He dares to be a fool, and that is the first step in the direction of wisdom."* [14]

—James G. Huneker

*"In wisdom gathered over time I have found that every experience is a form of exploration."* [15]

—Ansel Adams

Understanding wisdom is traced to the griots of old, the Sanskrit of yesteryear, and the ancestral rhythms of those seeking ways of existence through a spirit of creativity to offer direction, guidance, and community building. As an artist, you, too, are a wisdom-bearer. However, getting to the point of wisdom on the lifespan is to relinquish fear, feel contentment with life, and impart *life lessons* to others on their journey.

## ACTIVITY: DARING TO BE A FOOL

Write down an instance today, in which you dared to be a fool. What did you learn? How has seeing yourself in a foolish way helped you to unlock the wisdom within?

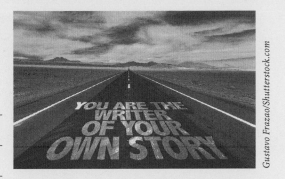

Gustavo Frazao/Shutterstock.com

_____

_____

_____

_____

_____

## ACTIVITY: TODAY'S EXPERIENCES

What have you experienced today? Can you tell it in a story? Or write it in a journal? Select one story, or an account of what occurred to you today. Describe the situation and what you did. Now that you have reflected on it and released the wisdom that you bear inside, what could you have done differently in the story? Be sure to acknowledge that you have wisdom. It's there for you to call upon when needed.

Sergey Nivens/Shutterstock.com

_____

_____

_____

_____

_____

# To Dare: Don't Be Afraid to Reach

*"A journey of a thousand miles begins with one step."* [16]

—Lao Tzu

Brian A Jackson/Shutterstock.com

Telling stories is at the very foundation of human behavior. We, as humans, learn how to express ourselves through the act of story. Stories tell about how we understand the world and how the world co-creates identity and meaning of the world with us. When we use stories as a way of knowing, it helps us to better understand and appreciate the creativity that lies at the foundation of storying our lived experiences.[17–20]

Personal narratives are integral to autobiographical memory and to identity, and are linked to positive development outcomes throughout the lifespan.[20–22] Go outside of your comfort zone. Engage others in the act of telling stories.[23] When you have developed trust, tell your story.

## ACTIVITY: SHARING YOUR SELF/SELVES

Think of an experience that best defines who you are in your life right now. Write down your personal narrative. In it, be sure to write what has been your challenge, and how are you daring yourself to face the challenge or the fear? Daring to face your fear is the unlocked door to artistry.

_____

_____

_____

_____

_____

# The Here and The Now

From infancy to adolescence, humans are in wonderment. This characteristic is truly the beauty of youth. As we age, the Universe challenges us to maintain and take hold of that wonderment each and every day, through the creative and artistic dimensions of narrative exploration.[24–26] We find a clue to link us to the rest of the world by living and staying in the moment. What this means, is to live *moment by moment*—not living in the past, while at the same time, not residing in the future. Ours is to live right now, right here—in the present moment. If we give our total energy to the life force of the here-and-now, then our totality of consumption of energy, intentionality, breath, senses, and pure focused wisdom is concentrated in the one instance we call a moment. It is then, that we are in our greatest moment—a moment of timelessness. Without constraints of time, truth can reveal itself and creativity abounds.

M.Photos/Shutterstock.com

## Conclusion

In this chapter you have learned how to embrace your own artistic prowess and to unlock its potential. The benefits of centering the body, breath control, and affirmations of self-confidence all unlock the hidden potential of the artist within. Moreover, we have discussed the ways in which the lifespan is a canvas for lived experience and telling our story shapes our identity. Grasping new ways of approaching mindfulness offer innovative choices for our health, wellness, life challenges, and life affirmations. Being present to our creativity from the wonderment of childhood to the wisdom of each stage of life development, means that we never lose the breath of life, when instantiated in the moment of artistic creativity. Kathe Kollwitz said it best in a charge to us all: "I do not want to die…until I have faithfully made the most of my talent and cultivated the seed that was placed in me until the last small twig has grown." [27]

## References

1. Davis, O. I. (2015). The artist within across the lifespan. In M. Napoli, *Whole person health mindfulness across the lifespan*. Dubuque: Kendall Hunt Publishers.

2. Davis, J. G. (2015). Personal interview. May, 2015. Phoenix, AZ.

3. Ellis, D. G. (1999). *Crafting society: Ethnicity, class, and communication theory*. Lawrence Erlbaum Associates: London.

4. Erikson, E. H. (1953). Growth and crises of the 'healthy personality.' *Psyche*, 7:1, 1–31.

5. Erickson, E. (1963). *The eight ages of man: Childhood and society*. New York: Norton.

6. Berk, L. (2001). *Development through the lifespan*. Pearson Education India.

7. Greenacre, P. (1967). The influence of infantile trauma on genetic patterns. *Psychic trauma*, 108–153.

8. Houston, M., & Davis, O. I. (2002). *Centering ourselves: African American feminist and womanist studies of discourse*. Cresskill: Hampton Press.

9. Davis-Berman, J., & Berman, D. (1998). Lifestories: Processing experience throughout the lifespan. *Clinical gerontologist*, 19:3, 3–11.

10. Greenacre, P. (1957). The childhood of the artist: Libidinal phase development and giftedness. *The psychoanalytic study of the child*, 12, 47–72.

11. Gawain, S. (1986). *Creative visualization*. Mill Valley, CA: Whatever Publishing.

12. Ochs, E., & Capps, L. (2009). *Living narrative: Creating lives in everyday storytelling*. Cambridge: Harvard University Press.

13. Cameron, J. (2005). *The artist's way*. New York: Penguin.

14. Huneker, J. G. Retrieved from http://quotes.quotesquiz.com/quote/authors/james-huneker

15. Adams, A. Retrieved from https://www.goodreads.com/author/quotes/12115.Ansel_Adams

16. Tsu, L. Retrieved from http://www.brainyquote.com/quotes/quotes/l/laotzu137141.html

17. Reese, E., Yan, C., Jack, F., & Hayne, H. (2010). Emerging identities: Narrative and self from early childhood to early adolescence. In *Narrative Development in Adolescence* (pp. 23–43). New York: Springer US.

18. Kenyon, G. M. (1996). The meaning/value of personal storytelling. *Aging and Biography: Explorations in Adult Development*, 21–38. New York : Springer US.

19. Davis, O. I. (2010). Health disparities in our community: Reflections in art and performance—A community based participatory approach. In C. McLean & R. Kelly (Eds.), *Creative arts in interdisciplinary practice: Inquiries for hope and change* (pp. 123–149). Calgary, Ontario, Canada: Detselig/Temeron Press.

20. Singer, J. A. (2004). Narrative identity and meaning making across the adult lifespan: An introduction. *Journal of Personality*, 72:3, 437–460.

21. Heckler, M., & Birch, C. (1997). Building bridges with stories. 8–15. In Leeming, D.A. (ed), Storytelling encyclopedia: Historical, cultural, and multiethnic approaches to oral traditions around the world. Arizona: Onyx Press.

22. McCabe, A., & Bliss, L. S. (2003). *Patterns of narrative discourse: A multicultural, life span approach*. Boston: Allyn & Bacon.

23. Reese, E., Haden, C. A., Baker-Ward, L., Bauer, P., Fivush, R., & Ornstein, P. A. (2011). Coherence of personal narratives across the lifespan: A multidimensional model and coding method. *Journal of Cognition and Development*, 12:4, 424–462.

24. Pratt, M. W., Norris, J. E., Arnold, M. L., & Filyer, R. (1999). Generativity and moral development as predictors of value-socialization narratives for young persons across the adult life span: from lessons learned to stories shared. *Psychology and Aging*, 14:3, 414.

25. Cohler, B. J. (1982). Personal narrative and life course. *Life Span Development and Behavior*, 4, 205–241.

26. Mayo, J. A. (2001). Life analysis: Using life-story narratives in teaching life-span developmental psychology. *Journal of Constructivist Psychology*, 14:1, 25–41.

27. Kollwitz, K. Retrieved from www.brainyquote.com/quotes/authors/k/kathe_kollwitz.html

# MINDFUL AWARENESS REFLECTION JOURNAL

Choose one mindful experience as you begin your reflection.

### Empathically Acknowledge

Describe your experience.

_____

_____

_____

### Intentional Attention

Describe what you noticed.

| Breath |
| --- |
| Body |
| Emotions |
| Thoughts |
| Senses |

### Accept Without Judgment

Describe judgment; acceptance.

_____

_____

_____

### Willingly Choose

Choose to purposely respond to your experience.

_____

_____

_____

### Mindful Mac Meditation

Describe your meditation experiences. What did you learn from your meditation experience?

_____

_____

_____

# Mindful Daily Journal

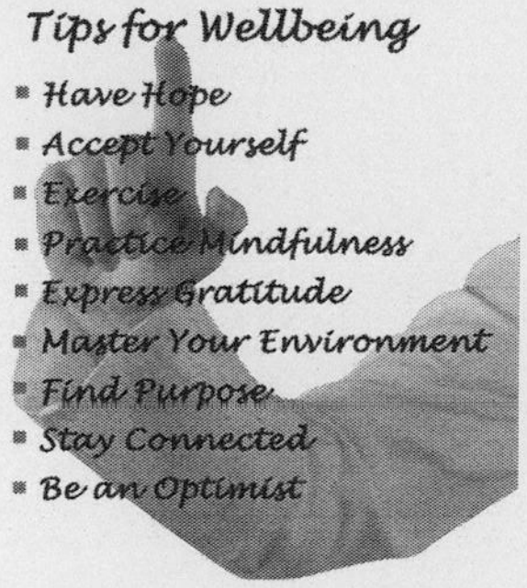

**TODAY'S Insight NOW!**

_____
_____
_____
_____

_____
_____
_____
_____
_____
_____
_____
_____
_____
_____
_____
_____
_____
_____
_____
_____
_____

*Tips for Wellbeing*

* Have Hope
* Accept Yourself
* Exercise
* Practice Mindfulness
* Express Gratitude
* Master Your Environment
* Find Purpose
* Stay Connected
* Be an Optimist

_____
_____
_____
_____

Date: _____     Make Today Count!

# Happiness:
# Journey and Destination

**Teri Kennedy**

*Photo courtesy of Maria Napoli*

*I take a step and begin to smile*

*With each step my smile grows*

*When I reach the top I'm grinning from ear to ear*

*My entire face is lit up with joy*

*It tickles my spirit*

*Happiness surrounds me*

Maria Napoli

Photograph courtesy of Teri Kennedy © Aisling West Publishing

What is happiness? Why is it important to whole person health? It has been said that "Happiness is a journey, not a destination."[1] Is it possible that it is both? Is happiness a state of being, something that can be actively pursued, or both?

## What Is Happiness?

When asked about the importance of personal happiness, individuals in the United States indicate that they think about happiness daily and that it is very important to them.[3] What is happiness and why is it so important to us? If we consult a dictionary, we'll gain insight into both the origin and meaning of happiness over time. Happiness is a noun originally meaning "good fortune: prosperity." It also means "a: a state of well-being and contentment: joy [and] b: a pleasurable or satisfying experience."[4] There is even a form referred to as felicity, which denotes "an intense form of happiness, bliss, or ecstasy."[4]

Now, if we take a little road trip in an imaginary time machine, we can trace the concept that we now refer to as *happiness* across time and cultures, dating from ancient Chinese and Greek philosophers to the present day. While ancient Chinese philosophers related happiness to good fortune, contemporary Americans tend to view happiness as something that can be actively pursued. Exploring the origins of this concept will facilitate our understanding of the various meanings of happiness and how we can seek to achieve it in our own lives.

The nearest Chinese equivalent of happiness, *fu* or *fu qi*, as well as the symbol of the bluebird representing happiness,[5] dates back to the Shang Dynasty (17th to 11th Century BC). The Shang Shu, or documents

Panu Ruangjan/Shutterstock.com

of the elder, related *fu* to longevity, prosperity, health, peace, virtue, and a comfortable death. A popular Chinese New Year greeting, "May the five fus come to your door," survives to this day. Fu was later extended to mean fortune, luck, and a life free of obstacles. [6] Modern Chinese language has three distinct words for happiness, ranging from the least to the longest lasting form: *gaoxìng* (least lasting; a momentary mood), *kuàilè* (extended lasting; related to special occasions), and *xìngfú* (long lasting feeling; often in the context of the family).[7] The Japanese conception of happiness involves good fortune. You may have seen a sculpture called a Maneki Neko, or beckoning cat, in a restaurant. It is believed that having this sculpture displayed in your business or home can bring wealth, good fortune, or customers.

Ancient Greek philosophers from Socrates through the Epicureans also contemplated the meaning of happiness. Aristippus of Cyrene, a student of Socrates, developed *hedonism*, the first complete philosophy of happiness in which the goal of life was to seek external pleasure.[8] Rather than external pleasures, Antisthenes praised the pleasures that spring from one's soul. He saw a life of peace, simplicity, naturalness, modesty, and virtue or mental work as the means of dissolving inner tensions and seeking inner happiness and enlightenment. Aristotle viewed the good life or *eudainomia*, trans-

lated as happiness, welfare, or human flourishing, as the ultimate aim of human thought and action.[9] Greek philosophers also shifted from a focus on the individual to society, inserting the notion of social justice as a means to achieve happiness. "For the Greeks, excellence could be manifest only in a city or a community…. A solitary person was not fully human…. It was only in a fair and just society that…men and women could be fully human—and happy."[10]

Now, let's re-board our time machine and fast forward in time. Contemporary Americans view happiness as something that can be actively pursued. John Locke (1632–1704) saw the pursuit of happiness as a necessity and the very foundation of liberty. He viewed happiness as not merely hedonistic, but as something that engaged the intellect and required careful discrimination between imaginary versus true happiness.[11] Thomas Jefferson wrote in 1819, "Happiness the aim of life. Virtue the foundation of happiness." He famously substituted the word "property" with "the pursuit of happiness,"[12] hence the phrase "Life, Liberty and the pursuit of Happiness" as unalienable rights in the United States Declaration of Independence.[13] As with the Greeks, the pursuit of happiness was not merely a matter of achieving individual pleasure. Happiness included the civic virtues of courage, moderation, and justice, and was referred to as *social happiness* by Alexander Hamilton and other founders.[14]

## Happiness as an Art and Science

The development of evolutionary psychology, which attempts to explain how our minds work in relation to the evolutionary challenges they were designed to solve, reinforced happiness as a concept that has endured across both time and cultures.[15] Early researchers like William James (1842–1910) recognized that psychology could be approached like anthropology and that it was important to study both *what* people think and *how* they think about their lives. In the 1960s, Paul Ekman identified a set of six basic emotions that are universally recognized (anger, fear, surprise, joy, disgust, and sadness), identified facial expressions

that accompanied these feelings, and found cross-cultural agreement for which feelings go along with various situations. A recent study using a Generative Facial Grammar platform claims that there are only four basic human facial expressions: happiness, sadness, fear/surprise, and anger/disgust.[16]

Psychologists in the 20th century primarily concentrated upon anxiety and depression to the neglect of focusing upon positive emotional states. The emphasis changed when it was found that positive and negative affect were independent from one another.[17] Consistent with the shift in focus from human unhappiness to happiness is the *strengths perspective.* While realistically recognizing issues and problems, it helps us focus upon and harness the strengths inherent in each of us. This approach provides a framework for "rediscovering the wholeness" of each person and provides a lens through which to view individuals, families, groups, and communities in a different way.

> All must be seen in the light of their capacities, talents, competencies, possibilities, visions, values, and hopes, however dashed and distorted these may have become through circumstance, oppression, and trauma. The strengths approach requires an accounting of what people know and what they can do…. It requires composing a roster of resources existing within and around the individual, family, or community.[18] (Saleebey, 1996, p. 297)

*Hedonics,* or the study of happiness[19], gained ground during the 1990s when a handful of maverick researchers set out to study human happiness and positive emotions.[20] In 1998, Dr. Martin Seligman dedicated his term as newly elected President of the American Psychiatric Association to the establishment of a new field, positive psychology.[21] By 2000, positive psychology had taken off and interdisciplinary and international research on happiness was being published in the *Journal of Happiness Studies.*[22] In research literature, happiness is generally defined as the presence of positive and absence of negative affect[23] and is used interchangeably with terms including well-being, subjective well-being, life satisfaction, and quality of life. Subjective well-being measures the cognitive and affective evaluations of our lives, assuming that the good life necessarily involves liking our life.[24]

In their seminal 1998 book, *The Art of Happiness: A Handbook for Living,* His Holiness the Dalai Lama and physician Howard Cutler explored mental health and human well-being by linking Buddhist philosophy with modern scientific theory. They saw happiness as an art, viewing the "concept of happiness as an achievable goal, something that we can deliberately cultivate through practice and effort". Their fundamental principle was that "[t]here is an inextricable link between one's personal happiness and kindness, compassion, and caring for others", citing studies demonstrating that happier people tended to be more caring and willing to reach out to and assist others. Further, they suggested that increased happiness could be experienced by intentionally practicing kindness and compassion.[25]

## Happiness Across the Life span

Studies of happiness, using measures of life satisfaction as a proxy for happiness, have been undertaken to see if there are any age-related changes across the life span using both cross-sectional studies, in which a group of individuals from different population groups or locations are observed at the same point in time, and longitudinal studies, in which the same group of people are observed at various points over a period of time, sometimes over several years. Longitudinal studies provide more solid support for the relationship between age and happiness.[26] Such studies involve cohorts, or people who share an historical event, such as being born in the same time period, or represent a sample population, for instance a representative sample of a specific country. Longitudinal studies have demonstrated that some aspects of subjective well-being increase as we age.

A national sample of Americans found an increase in positive affect and decrease in negative affect across age cohorts, with some differences depending upon gender and personality.[27] Another study found a positive correlation between age and life satisfaction in adults ranging in age from 25 to 75 years.[28] Let's unpack this further and find out what we know about happiness at each developmental stage of our lives.

*Mopic/Shutterstock.com*

## Infancy

If you have spent any time around infants, you have likely experienced the exchange of smiles between a parent and their baby. A smiling adult face can elicit a smiling response from an infant. Infants as young as seven months of age are able to distinguish facial expressions representing happiness from those displaying fear or anger.[29] Research has found that facial expressions displaying happiness are evident from early childhood and are coded by the age of five.[30] Toddlers, even before the age of two, exhibit more happiness when sharing a treat with others than when receiving a treat, particularly in an act of "costly giving" in which they are "forfeiting their own resources."[31]

*SvetlanaFedoseyeva/Shutterstock.com*

## Early and Middle Childhood

As early as age three to four, children begin associating colors with emotional states, with happiness most often associated with the color yellow.[32] Although we've pointed out that facial expressions representing happiness appear by early childhood, it's important to note that smiling is not always related to happiness in children. Excessive displays of smiling can also represent nervousness or efforts to please or ingratiate others.[33]

Childhood happiness is related to events that occur in the child's life. Events recalled by adults that were more highly correlated with childhood unhappiness included feeling unloved and being the recipient of physical and sexual abuse, as well as severe criticism. In fact, "unkind actions and words toward children" were more predictive of childhood unhappiness than the death of a parent, proving that words do hurt as much as sticks and stones. The good news is that unhappiness in childhood does not doom an adult to unhappiness, in fact approximately two thirds of adults who reported having very unhappy or unhappy childhoods claimed to be happy or very happy in adulthood.[34] This demonstrates the power of the human spirit to overcome adversity, also known as *resilience.*

Happiness is associated with social relationships in children ages 9 to 12, including positive interactions with family and friends.[35] Up to 16.5% of happiness in children of this age can be explained by spirituality.[36] Possessing high self-esteem, an internal locus of control, and a stable emotional temperament has been shown to be related to high life satisfaction or perceived quality of life (PQOL) among children.[37] A

*marekuliasz/Shutterstock.com*

*Poznyakov/Shutterstock.com*

study to determine what children say when asked makes them happy found that third and fourth graders were more likely to include hobbies and less likely to include material items than were older children.[38]

Is there any relationship between happiness and the way we learn in school? Japanese philosophers Tsunesaburo Makiguchi, Josei Toda, and Daisaku Ikeda argued that "happiness must form the fundamental principle of all learning programs." In keeping with this belief, a group of Japanese early childhood educators contended that happiness was the most important consideration for quality learning in early childhood.[39]

# Adolescence

Extraversion among adolescents is a strong predictor of happiness. Variables that both predict and influence happiness include friendship and self-confidence, as evidenced by self-evaluated academic performance rather than actual grades. Although happiness and loneliness are negatively correlated, it is important to note that the presence or absence of factors that predict happiness do not necessarily suggest the prospect of loneliness, nor is the opposite true.[40]

The importance of friendship to self-reported happiness reflects the importance of peer relationships at this stage of life. Peers provide the benefits of social networks including "shared interest[s] and enjoyable activities, positive feedback, [and] social support."[41]

*Artens/Shutterstock.com*

When asked what made them happy, seventh and eighth graders were more likely to respond that people, pets, and material things made them happy than were younger or older children. Those in eleventh and twelfth grade were more likely to consider achievements as making them happy than were younger children. This was closely followed by people and pets, again acknowledging the importance of social relationships at this age.[42]

# Young Adulthood

According to Erik Erikson, young adulthood is the stage of psychosocial development during which we are seeking resolution of the conflict between intimacy and isolation. Those who successfully resolve this stage are able to seek out and secure a meaningful relationship with a partner, becoming intimate with one another while maintaining their individual identities. Failure to resolve this conflict can result in isolation and the lack of a meaningful, close relationship.[43] Among adults, happiness has been "associated with personality traits, living conditions, self-esteem, feeling in love, democracy...[and] with specific loci of brain activity." [44]

Happiness has an interesting and unexpected relationship to socioeconomic status and income, referred to as the *happiness-income paradox.* Over the past 50 years, while the per capita income has risen dramatically in developed countries, there has not been an associated increase in measures of average happiness.[45] As it turns out, autonomy is a stronger predictor of happiness than income and is related to improved health. In fact, autonomy accounts for 20 times more variation in the level of happiness than income. In 2009 dollars, an additional $10,000 in income only resulted in a 2% increase in the likelihood of being happy. In fact, a much more effective predictor of happiness than earning more income is actually having friends and relatives who are happy.[46]

Often viewed as a component of good mental health, happiness or life satisfaction considers whether one finds life "interesting, happy, easy, or lonely", and has been found to predict lower mortality. [47] An interesting, happy life involves creating meaning. Having a sense of meaningfulness and hope has been found to be related to subjective well-being as a proxy for happiness among university students. Students who were more hopeful were also more grateful for what they had in life and more forgiving of others when encountering conflict.[48]

It's important to differentiate meaning from happiness. Situated within early adulthood is the *parenthood paradox,* so named because while parents self-report satisfaction with having children, they simultaneously score low on happiness measures. Parental satisfaction is likely connected to an increase in parental meaning, but it accompanies a reduction in parental happiness.[49]

## Middle Adulthood

Erikson described middle adulthood as a time during which individuals are seeking to resolve the conflict between generativity and stagnation. Those who successfully address this challenge are invested in the well-being of others and involved with their families, work, and communities. Those who remain stagnated are not productive and can become absorbed in themselves and their immediate environment.[50] Generativity seeks to provide for the next generation and has a positive association with happiness as indicated by measures of life satisfaction.[51] Those who don't apply this drive to their own children or families may direct their energies through altruistic or creative outlets.[52]

In middle adulthood, children begin to leave home and parents become *empty nesters.* This stage is accompanied by an increase in life satisfaction associated with improvements in marital happiness, which is strongest right after the departure of the children. Two possible conditions support a significant improvement in overall satisfaction with life: regular contact with the children who left home or the continued presence of young teens in the home; both are related to the importance of the parental role to a continuing sense of well-being.[53] Among

women in middle adulthood, generativity was associated with role satisfaction as a partner and parent, and contributed to successful aging and life satisfaction.[54]

Humans are meaning-makers. Happiness may be the spoken goal, but it results from involvement in meaningful relationships and activities. When asked what gives meaning to life, it's common to respond by sharing a list of "goals, wishes, and dreams for the future." This striving toward goals is seen as critical to happiness and "the good life". Recognition of the relationship between happiness and life satisfaction has led to the development of a number of individual and group counseling approaches (e.g., quality of life therapy, well-being therapy, meaning-centered counseling, and goal-focused group psychotherapy), each designed to support the achievement and revision of goals and priorities, thereby providing meaning and structure to life.[55]

# Late Adulthood

Late adulthood has been divided into the young-old (ages 65–74), middle-old (ages 75–84), and oldest-old (85 years and older).[56] In late adulthood, we enter Erikson's final stage of development during which individuals seek to resolve the conflict between integrity versus despair.[57] Integrity involves "acceptance of one's own and only life cycle and of the people who have become significant to it as something that had to be…and an acceptance that one's life is one's responsibility."[58] Successful completion of this stage leads to an integrated sense of self involving personal satisfaction and a sense of peace and well-being. Failure to resolve this stage results in despair over lost opportunities in life.[59]

Autonomy, which we first met in early and middle adulthood, surfaces again in late adulthood as important to a sense of life satisfaction and happiness. A survey conducted by AARP found that 90% of individuals age 65 and over prefer to remain in their own homes, also referred to as aging in place.[60] Here autonomy is expressed as a desire to be in control of our own decisions and destiny, and as a strong expression of the importance of maintaining a sense of home and place. For those individuals who require assisted, congregate, or institutional living, autonomy continues to be important. Supporting quality of life for individuals living in these circumstances involves maximizing choice whenever and wherever possible, even in seemingly small areas of daily life like having a choice between two entrees at dinner. A study of older adults living in rural Chile found a significant relationship between individual happiness and food, specifically the frequency of eating with companions for women, self-perceived health, and functionality.[61]

An important task in late adulthood involves meaning-making, providing an opportunity to reflect upon and take an inventory of what has been accomplished in life and weaving the threads of our lives into a tapestry of meaning. Viktor Frankl, who survived the ravages of life in a Nazi concentration camp during World War II, saw the search for meaning as our "primary motivational force."[62] Meaning and hope are associated with increased life satisfaction and improved health.[63] Older adults unable to continue to live independently can find sources of meaning while receiving long term care and services, where supporting quality of life includes things most of us take for granted like privacy, intimacy and sexual expression, security, and a sense of control of our daily routine.[64]

Our search for purpose and meaning facilitates a sense of spiritual well-being, which is linked to positive health outcomes. Research has shown that spirituality plays a critical role in the ability of older adults to live a life filled with happiness, satisfaction, and quality of life, with the added benefit of longevity.[65] People who are more spiritual are more hopeful, satisfied with their lives, and healthier, and maintain higher quality relationships with others.[66]

Aging occurs at different rates depending upon our genetics, lifestyle, and life circumstances including health disparities, which is represented by the difference between *chronological* versus *functional* aging. All 70 years olds share the same chronological age. Each is different from the other in terms of functional age. One 70 year old may be in exceptional health, teaching a yoga class at a local health center and, therefore, for all intents and purposes may be functioning as if they were 50 years of age. Another 70 year old may have been a lifelong smoker and lived a sedentary lifestyle and, therefore, may be functioning as if they were 90 years old. A 50-year-old American Indian male raised in poverty and living in an urban area away from the supportive culture of his tribal community might be functionally equivalent to a 70 year old, an example of a *health disparity*. A large scale study of a cohort observed over a 23 year period found a decline in negative affect, albeit at a slower pace, among the oldest group, and relative stability in positive affect, with a slight decline among the oldest group.[67] These late life reductions in levels of life satisfaction can be related to declines in health, income, and social supports.[68]

PedroMatos/Shutterstock.com

To promote happiness and quality of life in our latter years, it is important that we maximize health and functional ability across the life span. This can be accomplished through universal access to whole person healthcare and supportive services, improved health literacy, a shift in focus from emergency and chronic care to prevention and early intervention, housing and public spaces that are accessible (also referred to as *visitable*), and communities that are age-friendly across the life cycle. Such a shift supports the concept of *active ageing*, defined by the World Health Organization as "the process of optimizing opportunities for health, participation and security in order to enhance quality of life as people age."[69] Active aging is also referred to as positive aging or *healthy aging*. Meaning and hope are both key factors in healthy aging.[70]

## Happiness and Whole Person Health

*"I have decided to be happy because it is good for one's health."*

—Voltaire

According to the World Health Organization, "Health is a state of complete physical, mental, and social well-being and not merely the absence of disease or infirmity."[71] It has been argued that this would better serve as a definition for happiness, whereas a narrower definition would suffice for health.[72]

Why is happiness important to whole person health? Self-reported happiness is strongly related to health. "Happy people live longer than unhappy people and are less vulnerable to disease."[73] In fact, happiness at one stage of life has been shown to be predictor of recovery time in response to health shocks, as well as relative health many years later. Researchers examined the autobiographical sketches of a group of nuns in the United States, written when they took their holy vows, rating the content for how many positive emotions they expressed compared to their life expectancies. Among the 25% of nuns who expressed the most positive emotions, 90% were still alive at age 85; while among the 25% who expressed the least positive emotions, only 34% were still alive at that age.[73]

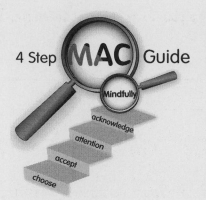

4 Step **MAC** Guide
Mindfully
acknowledge
attention
accept
choose

There is a strong association between happiness and mental health. It is thought that asking people if they are happy could aid in determining the care needs for individuals with mental health issues and that self-reports of happiness could measure the outcome of health-related interventions.[74]

Happiness doesn't predict longevity in sick populations, but has been found to be predictive of longevity in healthy populations. While it doesn't cure illness, happiness protects against becoming ill. In fact, the effect of happiness on longevity in healthy populations is remarkably strong, comparable to the impact of smoking versus not smoking on one's health.[75]

# Promoting Whole Person Health by Fostering Happiness

Since happiness is strongly associated with health, it would seem to be in our best interest to identify strategies to foster happiness as a means to improve our own health. Research can guide us to a variety of practices that have been found to foster self-reported increases in happiness and health including leisure activities, practicing gratitude, altruism and volunteering, spirituality, forgiveness, reminiscence, and social connections.

# Leisure Activities

Leisure activities have been demonstrated to produce short-term benefits to physical fitness and long-term benefits to physical health. Additionally, leisure experiences produce short-term gains in positive mood and satisfaction, as well as long-term gains in happiness, mental health, and social integration.[76] In people who participate in teams, positive mood was found to be associated with greater altruistic behavior, increased creativity, and more efficient decision-making, which contributed to changes in enhanced team performance. There was a strong association between a team member's own happiness and that of their teammates, and when a player's teammates were happier, the team's performance improved.[77]

*Monkey Business Images/Shutterstock.com*

## ACTIVITY: LEISURE

List three leisure activities you enjoy:

1. _____

2. _____

3. _____

Are you currently participating in these activities? If not, develop a plan to become re-involved or identify a new activity in which you would find enjoyment.

_____

_____

_____

# Gratitude

Gratitude has been found to have a connection to well-being, a proxy for happiness. A study of undergraduate students found a relationship between gratitude, self-esteem, social support, and life satisfaction, the latter of which is also a proxy for happiness.[78] Social support has been found to mediate the association between gratitude and depression in undergraduate students.[79] Gratitude enhanced the well-being of athletes, perhaps by eliciting more social support from team members and coaches.[80] It is thought that gratitude improves well-being by broadening "momentary repertoires of cognition and behavior" while building "enduring social and personal resources" (218).[81]

## ACTIVITY: GRATITUDE

List three people or things for which you are grateful:

1. _____

2. _____

3. _____

In what ways could you express your gratitude? (Be specific.)

_____

_____

_____

_____

_____

Hannamariah/Shutterstock.com

# Altruism and Volunteering

You may recall *Pay It Forward,* a novel by Catherine Ryan Hyde and a film by the same name, in which an 11-year-old boy launches a good will movement as a result of an assignment by his social studies teacher: think of an idea to change the world for the better. The idea of paying it forward involves the ethic of reciprocity, repaying an act of kindness with kindness, harkening back to the Golden Rule. *Altruism* and *volunteering* exemplify an attitude and act of kindness, respectively. Altruistic emotions and compassionate behaviors have been shown to have positive associations with well-being, happiness, health, and longevity, so long as the individual wasn't overwhelmed with the helping tasks at hand.[82] People who volunteer are healthier and happier than those who don't. These individuals also benefit from rich social connections derived from belonging to community organizations.[83]

## ACTIVITY: PAY IT FORWARD

Describe your plan to *Pay It Forward?*

_____

_____

_____

_____

What specific steps would you need to take to implement your plan?

_____

_____

_____

_____

Who else would you need to involve?

_____

_____

_____

_____

What resources would you need to secure?

_____

_____

_____

_____

*Andy Dean Photography/Shutterstock.com*

## Spirituality

Spirituality, defined as "a sense of transcendence beyond one's immediate circumstances", relates to our sense of purpose, meaning, and integration, as well as the availability of inner resources of support.[84] While spirituality can include adherence to a specific religious tradition, it can also involve holding a philosophical belief that serves as an organizing principal in life, with or without a belief in a power greater than ourselves. Spirituality promotes happiness through its relationship to improved physical and mental health, subjective well-being, life satisfaction, and quality of life. In fact, there is "overwhelming evidence of positive health outcomes linked to spirituality."[85]

Participation in religious services and the degree to which one is affiliated with their religious tradition are both positively associated with happiness, as measured by subjective well-being.[86] A significant association exists between religiosity and happiness. This relationship held constant both in studies comparing attitudes between Christianity and Judaism, as well as with individuals ranging in age from their late teens to their late seventies. It has been suggested that this association relates to "psychological well-being, which is thought to reflect human development, positive functioning and existential life challenges"[87] The Dalai Lama saw spirituality, along with kindness, tolerance, and forgiveness, as part of the art of happiness and the development of a positive, constructive state of mind.[88] Research demonstrates that "spirituality, perceived meaning of life and hope are significant predictors of psychological well-being."[89]

*STILLFX/Shutterstock.com*

## SPIRITUAL INVENTORY

The World Health Organization developed an instrument called the *WHOQOL Spirituality, Religiousness, and Personal Beliefs (SRPB) Field-Test Instrument*. The entire instrument is composed of 132 questions.

To complete the inventory, go to: http://www.who.int/mental_health/media/en/622.pdf

Respond to the questions related to how your personal beliefs affect your quality of life on page 19.

Next, respond to the questions about your spiritual, religious, or personal beliefs and how they affect your quality of life on pages 20-23.

What have you learned about your personal beliefs after completing these questions?

_____

_____

_____

How can this knowledge help you improve the quality of your life?

_____

_____

_____

# Forgiveness

Forgiveness is a process by which we can let go of the shackles that bind our hearts to hurt. Forgiveness doesn't mean that we forget the act, but that we forgive the actor and separate the person from the behavior. Hanging onto anger and hate festers negative emotions and can lead to stress and illness. When we hold onto these emotions, we are only hurting ourselves. Letting go of these negative emotions can reduce our stress and foster healing.

Forgiveness is central to the concept of *restorative justice*, "a response to criminal behavior that seeks to restore the losses suffered by crime victims and to facilitate peace and tranquility among opposing parties."[90] Restorative justice focuses upon repair, encounter, and transformation.[91] Forgiveness leads to happiness and promotes social harmony.[92] Happiness was treated as a trait difference in one study and as an emotional state difference in another study. When treated as a trait difference, highly happy people were more willing to forgive murderers when either ingroup or outgroup members were killed than were very unhappy people. When treated as an emotional state difference, happiness was found to bring more forgiveness when both ingroup or outgroup members were harmed than was sadness, with sad participants forgiving less when ingroup members were harmed versus outgroup members.[93]

## ACTIVITY: FORGIVENESS

What hurts am I hanging onto?

_____

_____

_____

Who do I need to forgive to move on and heal?

_____

_____

_____

Write a letter to the individual you would like to forgive. Focus on their actions without judgment, and describe how these actions affected you. Tell the individual that you forgive them. Forgive yourself for harboring anger and hate, then let go of these negative emotions.

DankaLilly/Shutterstock.com

You may choose to deliver the letter to the individual or tear it up and confidentially dispose of it.

# Reminiscence

The act of reminiscence, or reviewing one's life, has been found to promote well-being and help establish and maintain a sense of personal identity in older adults. It can provide a positive experience by bolstering self-esteem or generating a sense of pleasure, and can help one cope with negative experiences by providing comfort or closure to painful events.[94]

Mutual or social reminiscence involves engaging in reminiscence with another person. While both older and younger adults benefitted from mutual reminiscence, older adults were able to derive stronger positive emotions, primarily related to positive events.[95] It was of note that more frequent participation in positive reminiscing was a predictor of perceived ability to enjoy life. While both the use of cognitive imagery and memorabilia led to an increase in the percentage of time individuals reported feeling happy over the previous week, those individuals who used cognitive imagery reported a greater ability to enjoy positive events than those who used memorabilia to reminisce.[96]

An excellent example of intergenerational mutual reminiscence can be found in the PhotoWings project of Dublin City University. Participants included pairs of traditional university students and older adult learners from the community who shared photographs around a theme. Pairs shared stories about their respective photographs, then reflected on and wrote stories about their experience. The stories were published on a project blog and both photographs and reflections were featured in an exhibit, attended by participants and the general community.[97] This strategy is an effective way to bring generations together to foster mutual happiness through reminiscence.

## ACTIVITY: PHOTO PROJECT

Contact an older family member, neighbor, or an area senior center or housing facility to make arrangements to visit an older adult. Select or take a photograph that reflects the meaning of "home" to you and ask the older adult to do the same. If they don't have access to photographs, pick up an inexpensive disposable camera or smart phone and assist them with using it to take photos that represent their ideas of "home." Compare your photographs, share your stories and ideas, and summarize your experience in writing.

Lisa S./Shutterstock.com

_____

_____

_____

_____

# Social Connections

The single most effective strategy for fostering happiness is through social connections. Researchers have found that happiness spreads from person to person through social networks. "Everything we do or say tends to ripple through our network."[98] Unhappy and happy people tend to cluster in separate groups, with unhappy people more likely to be at the periphery of the network.

According to the *Three Degrees of Separate Rule,* the fewer the degrees of separation of social relationships, the more likely the people in the network were to be happy regardless of other circumstances. A person was 15% more likely to be happy if a person connected to them by one degree of separation was also happy. The effect was reduced to 10% at two degrees, and 6% at three degrees, waning to no measurable effect at four degrees of separation. As it turned out, the key determinant for happiness was "the happiness of others."[98]

*Sergey Novikov/Shutterstock.com*

## ACTIVITY: SOCIAL CONNECTIONS

List five friends whom you consider to be happy and their degree of relationship to you:

| Friend | Degree(s) of Separation |
|--------|-------------------------|
|        |                         |
|        |                         |
|        |                         |
|        |                         |
|        |                         |

What are some specific ways in which you could increase your exposure to the happy people in your life?

_____

_____

_____

_____

_____

# Mindfulness and Happiness

*"Happiness is like a butterfly which, when pursued, is always beyond our grasp, but, if you will sit down quietly, may alight upon you."*

—Anonymous

Photograph courtesy of Teri Kennedy © Aisling West Publishing

We can foster happiness by living mindfully and engaging in mindfulness-based practices, including mindful meditation. Additionally, the visual and expressive arts offer a pathway to happiness including writing, music, art, and dance.

## Mindfulness Meditation

Meditation has been shown to have a positive effect on subjective well-being, and therefore happiness. Those who meditate regularly experience reduced levels of negative emotion. A course in mindfulness meditation was shown to reduce stress, increase well-being, and improve immune responses.[99] Older adults living with depression, anxiety, or both were enrolled in a group using a mindfulness-based version of a technique called cognitive therapy, which is based on the notion that our perceptions of situations impact our emotional responses to those situations.[100] This mindful approach was found to be effective in reducing symptoms of depression and anxiety, negative thoughts, and problems with sleep.[101]

## The Arts

According to the *National Core Arts Standards: A Conceptual Framework for Arts Learning* by the National Coalition for Core Arts Standards, the arts are valued as a means to well-being, therefore happiness. "The arts enrich mental, physical, and emotional well-being and should be encouraged as a means of enjoyment and stimulation."[102]

2xSamara.com/Shutterstock.com

EdBockStock/Shutterstock.com

## Writing

The process of regularly writing about one's experiences has been found to have a positive effect on well-being, health, and immune function. These benefits held whether an individual was writing about positive or negative experiences. Findings suggest that writing may be another form of mindful practice, allowing us to be aware of and detach from our thoughts.[103]

De-V/Shutterstock.com

## Music

Music has positive effects on our sense of well-being, and therefore our sense of happiness. This holds true whether we actually listen to music or imagine music or rhythm. Music impacts even more areas of our brain than language, releasing hormones that have positive effects on our mood, happiness, and bodies.[104]

Ollyy/Shutterstock.com

# Happiness: A Journey and a Destination

*Happiness—the path.*
*Each step a destination*
*along the journey.*

—Teri Kennedy

*Photograph courtesy of Teri Kennedy*
*© Aisling West Publishing*

According to Alfred D. Souza:

> Happiness is a journey, not a destination. For a long time it seemed to me that life was about to begin—real life. But there was always some obstacle in the way, something to be gotten through first, some unfinished business, time still to be served, a debt to be paid. At last it dawned on me that these obstacles were my life. This perspective has helped me to see there is no way to happiness. Happiness is the way. So treasure every moment you have and remember that time waits for no one.[105]

In reflecting upon this quotation, we can't find the path to happiness. Happiness *is* the path! Finding happiness requires us to remove the obstacles that make up our lives and find the path that has been there all along. We need to learn what we can do to facilitate the journey.

I would differ from Souza in that I believe that happiness is both a journey and a destination. If we slow down our thinking and approach our journey, mindfully aware of each step and being fully present in the moment, each step is in fact its own destination. We then move on to the next step, the next destination, and so forth. Just like the butterfly at the beginning of this chapter, the more we pursue the path, the more it eludes us. We must approach happiness quietly, be mindfully aware, and the path will be revealed to us. Rather than pursue the path, we must focus on this moment and savor each step along the way!

Photograph courtesy of Teri Kennedy © Aisling West Publishing

# References (Endnotes)

1. Souza, A. D. (2015) *Good reads.* Retrieved from https://www.goodreads.com/quotes/ 620943 -happiness-is-a-journey-not-a-destination-for-a-long

2. H.H. Dalai Lama, & Cutler, H. C. (2009). *The art of happiness: A handbook for living* (10th Anniversary Ed.). New York, NY: Riverhead Books.

3. Freedman, 1978; Diener, Suh, Smith, & Shao, 1995; & Triandis, Bonempo, Leung, & Hui, 1990 as cited in Lynubomirsky, S., Sheldon, K. M., & Schkade, D. (2005, June 1). Pursuing happiness: The architecture of sustainable change. *Review of General Psychology,* 9(2), 111–131. UC Riverside: Retrieved from: http://escholarship.org/uc/item/4v03h9gv

4. Merriam-Webster, Incorporated. (2015). Happiness. *Merriam-Webster Dictionary.* Retrieved from http://www.merriam-webster.com/dictionary/happiness

5. Welch, P.B. (2008). Chinese art: A guide to motifs and visual imagery. Tokyo, Japan: Tuttle Publishing.

6. Lu, L. Understanding happiness: A look into the Chinese folk psychology. (2001). *Journal of Happiness Studies,* 2, 407–432.

7. Djuanda, S. (2013, October 14). Chinese word for happiness: The differences of Gaoxìng, Kuàilè and Xìngfú. Retrieved from http://www.brighthubeducation.com/ learning-chinese/97597-the-three-ways-to-express-happiness-in-chinese/

8. Moore, A. (2012) Hedonism. *The Stanford Encyclopedia of Philosophy* (Winter 2012 Edition), Edward N. Zalta (ed.). Retrieved from http://plato.stanford.edu/entries/hedonism/

9. (2015, March 9). Philosophy of happiness. *Wikipedia.* Retrieved from http://en.wikipedia.org/ wiki/Philosophy_of_happiness

10. Townsend, K. K. (2011, June 20). The pursuit of happiness: What the founders meant—and didn't. *The Atlantic.* Retrieved from http://www.theatlantic.com/business/archive/2011/06/ the-pursuit-of-happiness-what-the-founders-meant-and-didnt/240708/

11. Locke, J. (1690). An essay concerning human understanding. London.

12. Hamilton, C. V. (2008). Why did Jefferson change "property" to the "pursuit of happiness"? *History News Network.* Seattle, WA: George Mason University. Retrieved from http://historynewsnetwork.org/article/46460

13. *Declaration of Independence.* (1776, July 4). The charters of freedom: A new world is at hand. Archives.gov http://www.archives.gov/exhibits/charters/declaration_transcript.html

14. Hamilton, C. V. (2008, January 27). Why did Jefferson change "property" to the "pursuit of happiness"? History News Network. Seattle, WA: George Mason University. Retrieved from http://historynewsnetwork.org/article/46460

15. Nettle, D. (2005). *Happiness: The science behind your smile.* New York, NY: Oxford University Press.

16. University of Glasgow. (n.d.). Written all over your face: Humans express four basic emotions rather than six, says new study. *University News.* Glasgow, Scotland: University of Glasgow. Retrieved from http://www.gla.ac.uk/news/headline_306019_en.html

17. Cheng, H., & Furnham, A. (2002). Personality, peer relations, and self-confidence as predictors of happiness and loneliness. *Journal of Adolescence, 25,* 327–339.

18. Saleebey, D. (1996, May). The strengths perspective in social work practice: Extensions and cautions. *Social Work 41*(3), 296–305.

19. Nettle, D. (2005). *Happiness: The science behind your smile.* New York, NY: Oxford University Press.

20. H.H. Dalai Lama, & Cutler, H. C. (2009). *The art of happiness: A handbook for living* (10th Anniversary Ed.). New York, NY: Riverhead Books.

21. H.H. Dalai Lama, & Cutler, H. C. (2009). *The art of happiness: A handbook for living* (10th Anniversary Ed.). New York, NY: Riverhead Books.

22. Nettle, D. (2005). *Happiness: The science behind your smile.* New York, NY: Oxford University Press.

23. Deci, E. L., & Ryan, R. M. (2008). Hedonia, eudaimonia, and well-being: An introduction. *Journal of Happiness Studies, 9,* 1–11.

24. Diener, E., Lucas, R. E., & Oishi, S. (2002). Chapter 5: Subjective well-being: The science of happiness and life satisfaction. 63–73. In C.R. Snyder & S. J. Lopez (Eds.), *Handbook of positive psychology.* New York, NY: Oxford University Press.

25. H.H. Dalai Lama, & Cutler, H. C. (2009). *The art of happiness: A handbook for living* (10th Anniversary Ed.). New York, NY: Riverhead Books, xx, xxvii.

26. Baird, B. M., Lucas, R. E., & Donnellan, M. B. (2010, November). Life satisfaction across the life span: Findings from two nationally representative panel studies. *Social Indicators Research, 99*(2), 183–203. doi:10.1007/s11205-010-9584-9

27. Mroczek, D. K., & Kolarz, C. M. (1998). The effect of age on positive and negative affect: A developmental perspective on happiness. *Journal of Personality and Social Psychology, 75,* 1333–1349. [PubMed: 9866191]

28. Prenda, K. M., & Lachman, M. E. (2001). Planning for the future: A life management strategy for increasing control and life satisfaction in adulthood. *Psychology and Aging, 16,* 206–216. [PubMed: 11405309]

29. Kestenbaum, R., & Nelson, C. A. (1990, October–December). The recognition and categorization of upright and inverted emotional expressions by 7 month-old infants. *Infant Behavior and Development, 12*(4), 497–511.

30. Rodger, H., Vizioli, L., Ouyang, X., & Caldara, R. (2015). Mapping the development of facial expression recognition. *Developmental Science.* doi: 10.1111/desc.12281

31. Aknin, L. B., Hamlin, J. K., & Dunn, E. W. (2012). Giving leads to happiness in young children. *PLoS ONE 7*(6), 1–4. e39211. doi:10.1371/journal.pone.0039211

32. Zentner, M. R. (2001). Preferences for colours and colour—emotion combinations in early childhood. *Developmental Science, 4,* 389–398. doi: 10.1111/1467-7687.00180

33. Biringen, Z., Robinson, J. L., & Emde, R. N. (2000). Appendix B: The emotional availability scales (3rd ed.; an abridged infancy/early childhood version). *Attachment & Human Development, 2*(2), 256–270.

34. Freeman, L. J., Templer, D. I., & Hill, C. (1999). The relationship between adult happiness and self-appraised childhood happiness and events. *The Journal of Genetic Psychology, 160*(1), 46–54.

35. Holder, M. D., & Coleman, B. (2009, June). The contribution of social relationships to children's happiness. *Journal of Happiness Studies, 10*(3), 329–349.

36. Holder, M. D., & Coleman, B. (2008). The contribution of temperament, popularity, and physical appearance to children's happiness. *Journal of Happiness Studies, 9*(2), 279–302.

37. Dew, T., & Huebner, E. S. (1994). Adolescents perceived quality of life: An exploratory investigation. *Journal of School Psychology, 32,* 185–199; Rigby, B., & Huebner, E. S. (2004). Do causal attributions mediate the relationship between personality and life satisfaction in adolescence? *Psychology in the Schools, 41,* 91–99.

38. Chapin, L. N. (2009). Please may I have a bike? Better yet, may I have a hug? An examination of children's and adolescents' happiness. *Journal of Happiness Studies, 10,* 541–562.

39. Ikegami, K., & Agbenyega, J. S. (2014, September). Exploring educators' perspectives: How does learning through 'happiness' promote quality early childhood education? [online]. *Australasian Journal of Early Childhood, 39*(3), 46-55. Retrieved from http://search.informit.com.au/documentSummary;dn=666548464454196;res=IELHSS> ISSN: 1836–9391

40. Cheng, H., & Furnham, A. (2002). Personality, peer relations, and self-confidence as predictors of happiness and loneliness. *Journal of Adolescence, 25,* 327–339.

41. Argyle, 1987, as cited in Cheng, H., & Furnham, A. (2002). Personality, peer relations, and self-confidence as predictors of happiness and loneliness. *Journal of Adolescence, 25,* 327–339.

42. Chapin, L. N. (2009). Please may I have a bike? Better yet, may I have a hug? An examination of children's and adolescents' happiness. *Journal of Happiness Studies, 10,* 541–562.

43. Erikson, E. (1950). *Childhood and society.* New York, NY: W. W. Norton.

44. Perneger, T. V., Hudelson, P. M., & Bovier, P. A. (2004). Health and happiness in young Swiss adults. *Quality of Life Research, 13,* 171–178.

45. Nettle, D. (2005). Happiness: *The science behind your smile.* New York, NY: Oxford University Press.

46. Christakis, N. A., & Fowler, J. H. (2009). *Connected: The surprising power of our social networks and how they shape our lives.* New York, NY: Little, Brown and Company.

47. Perneger, T. V., Hudelson, P. M., & Bovier, P. A. (2004). Health and happiness in young Swiss adults. *Quality of Life Research, 13,* 171–178.

48. Slezáčková, A. (2015). *Spirituality and Meaningfulness: Key Components of Mental Health and Happiness.* Keynote address. 50th National and International Conference of the Indian Academy of Applied Psychology, Tirupati, Andra Pradesh, India.

49. Baumeister, R. F. (1992). *Meanings of life.* Hillsdale, NJ: Erlbaum.

50. Erikson, E. (1950). *Childhood and society.* New York, NY: W. W. Norton.

51. McAdams, D. P., de St. Aubin, E., & Logan, R. L. (1993, June). Generativity among young, midlife, and older adults. *Psychology and Aging, 8*(2), 221–230.

52. Erikson, E. H. (1959). *Identity and the life cycle.* New York, NY: W. W. Norton and Company.

53. White, L., & Edwards, J. N. (1990, April). Emptying the nest and parental well-being: An analysis of national panel data. *American Psychological Review, 55*(2), 235–242.

54. Peterson, B. E., & Duncan, L. E. (2007, September). Midlife women's generativity and authoritarianism: Marriage, motherhood, and 10 years of aging. *Psychology and Aging, 22*(3), 411–419.

55. Emmons, R. A. (2003). Personal goals, life meaning, and virtue: Wellsprings of a positive life. *Flourishing: Positive psychology and the life well-lived,* 105–128.

56. Rogers, A. T. (2013). *Human behavior in the social environment* (3rd ed.). New York, NY: Routledge.

57. Erikson, E. (1950). *Childhood and society.* New York, NY: W. W. Norton.

58. Erikson, E. H. (1959). *Identity and the life cycle.* New York, NY: W. W. Norton and Company, 104.

59. Erikson, E. (1950). *Childhood and society.* New York, NY: W. W. Norton.

60. Farber, N., Shinkle, D., Lynott, J., Fox-Grage, W., & Harrell, R. (2011, December). *Aging in place: A state survey of livability policies and practices.* Washington, DC: National Conference of State Legislators & AARP Public Policy Institute.

61. Lobos, G., Grunert, K. G., Bustamante, M., & Schnettler, B. (2015, May). With health and good food, great life! Gender differences and happiness in Chilean rural older adults. *Social Indicators Research.* doi: 10.1007/s11205-015-0971-0

62. Frankl, V. E. (1959). *Man's search for meaning: An introduction to logotherapy.* New York, NY: Pocket Books, 154.

63. Slezáčková, A. (2015). *Spirituality and Meaningfulness: Key Components of Mental Health and Happiness.* Keynote address. 50th National and International Conference of the Indian Academy of Applied Psychology, Tirupati, Andra Pradesh, India.

64. Seeber, J. J. (2000). Meaning in long term care settings: Victor Frankl's contribution to gerontology. In M. E. Kimble (Ed.), *Victor Frankl's contribution to spirituality and aging* (pp. 141–157). New York, NY: The Haworth Pastoral Press.

65. Titiksha, C., Shubha, D., & Krishna K, S. (2015). Spiritual wellbeing and quality of life: A perspective in ageing. *Research Journal of Recent Sciences, 4,* 246–249.

66. Slezáčková, A. (2015). *Spirituality and Meaningfulness: Key Components of Mental Health and Happiness.* Keynote address. 50th National and International Conference of the Indian Academy of Applied Psychology, Tirupati, Andra Pradesh, India.

67. Charles, S. T., Reynolds, C. A., & Gatz, M. (2001). Age-related differences and change in positive and negative affect over 23 years. *Journal of Personality and Social Psychology, 80,* 136–151. [PubMed: 11195886]

68. Baltes, P. B., & Mayer, K. U. (1999). *The Berlin aging study: Aging from 70 to 100.* Cambridge, United Kingdom: Cambridge University Press.

69. World Health Organization. (2015). *Ageing and life course: What is "active ageing"?* Geneva, Switzerland: World Health Organization, para 1. Retrieved from http://www.who.int/ageing/active_ageing/en/

70. Slezáčková, A. (2015). *Spirituality and Meaningfulness: Key Components of Mental Health and Happiness.* Keynote address. 50th National and International Conference of the Indian Academy of Applied Psychology, Tirupati, Andra Pradesh, India.

71. Preamble to the Constitution of the World Health Organization as adopted by the International Health Conference, New York, 19–22 June, 1946; signed on 22 July 1946 by the representatives of 61 States (Official Records of the World Health Organization, no. 2, p. 100) and entered into force on 7 April 1948. Retrieved from http://www.who.int/about/definition/en/print.html

72. Saracci, R., (1997). The world health organisation needs to reconsider its definition of health. *British Medical Journal, 314,* 1409.

73. Danner, Snowden, & Friesen, 2001 as cited in Nettle, D. (2005). *Happiness: The science behind your smile.* New York, NY: Oxford University Press, 2.

74. Perneger, T. V., Hudelson, P. M., & Bovier, P. A. (2004). Health and happiness in young Swiss adults. *Quality of Life Research, 13,* 171–178.

75. Veenhoven, R. (2008). Healthy happiness: Effects of happiness on physical health and the consequences for preventive health care. *Journal of Happiness Studies, 9,* 449–469.

76. Lu, L., & Hu, C.H. (2005). Personality, leisure experiences and happiness. *Journal of Happiness Studies, 6,* 325–342.

77. Christakis, N. A., & Fowler, J. H. (2009). *Connected: The surprising power of our social networks and how they shape our lives.* New York, NY: Little, Brown and Company.

78. Kong, F., Ding, K., & Zhao, J. (2015). The relationship among gratitude, self-esteem, social support and life satisfaction among undergraduate students. *Journal of Happiness Studies, 16,* 477–489.

79. Wood, A. M., Maltby, J., Gillett, R., Linley, P. A., & Joseph, S. (2008). The role of gratitude in the development of social support, stress, and depression: Two longitudinal studies. *Journal of Research in Personality, 42,* 854–871.

80. Chen, L. H., Chen, M. Y., & Tsai, Y. M. (2012). Does gratitude always work? Ambivalence over emotional expression inhibits the beneficial effect of gratitude on well-being. *International Journal of Psychology, 47,* 381–392.

81. Fredrickson, B. L. (2001). The role of positive emotions in positive psychology: The broaden-and-build theory of positive emotions. *American Psychologist, 56,* 218–226.

82. Christakis, N. A., & Fowler, J. H. (2009) *Connected: The surprising power of our social networks and how they shape our lives.* New York, NY: Little, Brown and Company.

83. Post, S. G. (2005, June). Altruism, happiness, and health: It's good to be good. *International Journal of Behavioral Medicine, 12*(2), 66–77.

84. Monod, S., Brennan, M., & Büla, C. J. (2011, November). Instruments measuring spirituality in clinical research: A systematic review. *Journal of General Internal Medicine, 26*(11), 1345–1357.

85. Titiksha, C., Shubha, D., Krishna K, S. (2015). Spiritual wellbeing and quality of life: A perspective in ageing. *Research Journal of Recent Sciences, 4,* 246–249.

86. Argyle, 2001; Diener et al., 1999, 2009; Ellison et al., 2001; Ferris, 2002; Francis et al., 2008; Hadaway, 1978; Hadaway & Roof, 1978; Inglehart, 2010; Maselko & Kubzansky, 2006.

87. Lewis, C. A., Maltby, J., & Day, L. (2005). Religious orientation, religious coping and happiness among UK adults. *Personality and Individual Differences, 38,* 1193–1202.

88. H.H. Dalai Lama, & Cutler, H. C. (2009). *The art of happiness: A handbook for living* (10th Anniversary Ed.). New York, NY: Riverhead Books.

89. Slezáčková, A. (2015). *Spirituality and Meaningfulness: Key Components of Mental Health and Happiness.* Keynote address. 50th National and International Conference of the Indian Academy of Applied Psychology, Tirupati, Andra Pradesh, India, para 1.

90. Minor, K. I., & Hudson, J. (1996). A theoretical study and critique of restorative justice. In B. Galaway & J. Hudson (Eds.), Restorative justice: International perspectives. Amsterdam, The Netherlands: Criminal Justice Press and Kugler Publications, 117.

91. Restorative Justice Online. (2015). Lesson 1: Definition. Retrieved from http://www.restorative-justice.org/university-classroom/01introduction/tutorial-introduction-to-restorative-justice/lesson-1-definition/lesson-1-definition

92. Nehela, B. (2014, November 13). *The Role of forgiveness in building social harmony in modern society.* Qatar Foundation Annual Research Conference Proceedings: Vol., SSPP0281. DOI: 10.5339/qfarc.2014.SSPP0281 Retrieved from http://www.qscience.com/doi/abs/10.5339/qfarc.2014.SSPP0281

93. Jiang, F., Yue, S., Lu, S., & Yu, G. (2015, April). Can you forgive? It depends on how happy you are. *Scandinavian Journal of Psychology. 56*(2), 182–188.

94. Butler, R.N. (1963). The life review: An interpretation of reminiscence in the aged. *Psychiatry, 26,* 65–76; Coleman, P.G. (1974). Measuring reminiscence characteristics from conversation as adaptive features of old age. *International Journal of Aging and Human Development, 5,* 281–294; Fallot, R.D. (1980). The impact on mood on verbal reminiscing in later adulthood. *International Journal of aging and Human Development, 10,* 385–400.

95. Pasupathi, M., & Carstensen. L. L. (2003). Age and emotional experience during mutual remi-niscing. *Psychology and Aging, 18,* 430–442.

96. Bryant, F. B., Smart, C. M., & King, S. P. (2005). Using the past to enhance the present: Boosting happiness through positive reminiscence. *Journal of Happiness Studies, 6,* 227–260.

97. Dublin City University. (2014). PhotoWings & AshokaU InSights Grant Winner: Dublin, Ireland: Dublin City University. Retrieved from https://vimeo.com/82348214

98. Christakis, N. A., & Fowler, J. H. (2009). *Connected: The surprising power of our social networks and how they shape our lives.* New York, NY: Little, Brown and Company, 28, 50.

99. Leung & Singhalm, 2004; Davidson et al., 2003, as cited in Nettle, D. (2005). *Happiness: The science behind your smile.* New York, NY: Oxford University Press.

100. Beck Institute for Cognitive Behavior Therapy. (n.d.) *Frequently asked questions.* Bala Cynwdy, PA: Beck Institute for CBT. Retrieved from http://www.beckinstitute.org/cognitive -behavioral-therapy/

101. Foulk, M. A., Ingersoll-Dayton, B., Kavanaugh, J., Robinson, E., & Kales, H.C. (2014). Mindful-ness-based cognitive therapy with older adults: An exploratory study. *Journal of Gerontological Social Work, 57,* 498–520.

102. Prior, J., & Powell, P. (2015). Chapter 9: Creative connections: Technology and the arts, 137–151. In R. Papa (Ed.) Media rich instruction: Connecting curriculum to all learners. New York, NY: Springer Science+Business Media.

103. Pennebaker, 1997; Burton & King, 2004 as cited in Nettle, D. (2005). *Happiness: The science behind your smile.* New York, NY: Oxford University Press.

104. Biset-Bentchikou, C. Estache, A., & Ginsburgh, V. (2013, May). *Happiness and music.* Retrieved from http://www.ecares.org/ecare/personal/ginsburgh/papers/biset-estache.pdf

105. Souza, A. D. (2015) *Good reads.* Retrieved from https://www.goodreads.com/quotes/620943 -happiness-is-a-journey-not-a-destination-for-a-long

# MINDFUL AWARENESS REFLECTION JOURNAL

4 Step **MAC** Guide

Choose one mindful experience as you begin your reflection.

### Empathically Acknowledge

Describe your experience.

_____

_____

_____

### Intentional Attention

Describe what you noticed.

| Breath |
|--------|
| Body |
| Emotions |
| Thoughts |
| Senses |

### Accept Without Judgment

Describe judgment; acceptance.

_____

_____

_____

### Willingly Choose

Choose to purposely respond to your experience.

_____

_____

_____

### Mindful Mac Meditation

Describe your meditation experiences. What did you learn from your meditation experience?

_____

_____

_____

TODAY'S insight NOW!

_____
_____
_____
_____
_____
_____
_____
_____
_____
_____
_____
_____
_____
_____
_____
_____
_____
_____
_____

*Tips for Wellbeing*

- Have Hope
- Accept Yourself
- Exercise
- Practice Mindfulness
- Express Gratitude
- Master Your Environment
- Find Purpose
- Stay Connected
- Be an Optimist

_____
_____
_____
_____

Date: _____ Make Today Count!

# Answers to Chapter Questions

## ANSWERS TO CHAPTER 1 QUESTIONS

1. **How long has mindfulness been around and what does it mean to be mindful?**

   Mindfulness has been around for a very long time and is the ability of being able to engage in the moment without judgment.

2. **What are five benefits of mindfulness and how do they positively affect behavior?**

   1) Increased attention span

   2) Insight

   3) Empathy

   4) Impulse control

   5) Fear regulation

   All of these benefits allow us the opportunity to learn how to respond versus react when placed in stressful situations

3. **What are the three major areas of the brain and how do they develop in a baby's brain?**

   Reptilian (Brainstem): developed at birth and controls autonomic features such as heart rate and respiration. Mammalian (Limbic): develops through childhood reaching completion by adolescence controlling emotions. Neocortex (thinking brain): the newest and last part of the brain to finish development where our critical thinking occurs.

4. **Why are teenagers so emotional?**

   Teenagers have a beautifully developed limbic system (emotions), but an incomplete neocortex (thinking) so though they feel with full intensity, they do not have the critical thinking skills readily available to temper those emotions.

5. **How does mindfulness help children?**

   It has been shown to reduce stress, anxiety, reactivity, and bad behavior, improve sleep and self-esteem, and bring about greater calmness, relaxation, the ability to manage behavior and emotions, self-awareness and empathy. It also has been shown to improve academic success and increased attention.

6. **Why does the sympathetic response take us away from mindfulness?**

When we are perceiving a real or imagined threat, the nervous system will activate the autonomic nervous system and prepare the body for flight, fight, or freeze. When this occurs, the immune and digestive systems are subdued and the brain also adjusts, disengaging the neocortex and engaging the limbic and brainstem. Physiologically, you are incapable of being mindful in this moment; it is purely about maintaining the integrity of the organism and escaping the threat (real or perceived).

7. **How does mindfulness help re-engage the parasympathetic nervous system?**

Mindfulness allows us to step back and objectively experience the situation without judgement rather than becoming the emotion of the situation, thus allowing the neocortex to come back online and sync with the other two sections (limbic and brainstem) of the brain.

8. **What are some benefits of mindfulness for adults?**

Sleep, stress hormone control, body regulation, and brain degradation. We become responsive vs reactive beings.

9. **What is diaphragmatic breathing?**

A deep breath that encompasses both the chest and the belly.

10. **What is the difference between mindfully eating a meal versus the normal way we eat?**

Mindful eating is mindfulness applied to the food experience; completely paying attention to the food, its smell, texture, and taste without distractors. Many times we eat mindlessly while being distracted by external stimuli such as technology, reading material, or other people.

## ANSWERS TO CHAPTER 2 QUESTIONS

1. **Define ego.**

Ego is the organized mediator between the person and their perception of, and adaptation to, reality. The ego is responsible for reality testing and one's sense of personal identity.

2. **By contrast, what is a mindful ego?**

A mindful ego employs the strategies of mindfulness to restructure the emotional impact on our ego.

3. **Compare and contrast IQ (Intelligence Quotient) and EQ (Emotion Quotient).**

Answers will vary.

4. **What are the four factors of Salovey and Mayer's model?**

Perceiving emotions, reasoning with emotions, understanding emotions and managing emotions

5. **What are the two chemicals released during periods of anxiety and stressful events that put our bodies in a reactive mode (fight or flight/sympathetic mode)?**

Epinephrine (adrenaline) and cortisol

6. **What are the two chemicals released in our bodies during parasympathetic mode?**

Dopamine and endorphins

## ANSWERS TO CHAPTER 3 QUESTIONS

1. **What is the definition of exercise?**

Exercise is a physical activity that is planned, structured, and repetitively performed for the purpose of conditioning a part of the body, and comprised of a series of movements done to become stronger and healthier.

2. **What is the difference between active and aerobic exercise?**

Active exercise is motion imparted to a part of the body by voluntary contraction and relaxation of its controlling muscles. Aerobic exercise is designed to increase oxygen consumption and improve functioning of the cardiovascular and respiratory systems.

3. **What are the potential benefits of outdoor versus indoor activities?**

Various potential answers.

4. **What are some benefits of childhood exercise?**

Various potential answers.

5. **What are some contributing factors to adult inactivity?**

Various potential answers.

6. **What are some low-impact exercises that older adults can participate in?**

Exercises using exercise bands, weight machines, hand-held weights, callisthenic exercises (body weight provides resistance to movement), digging, lifting, and carrying as part of gardening, carrying groceries, yoga exercises, Tai chi exercises, walking.

7. **What three things will having a well-balanced, healthy diet with proper hydration do?**

1) Facilitate an effective exercise regimen, 2) reduce injuries, and 3) promote recovery

# ANSWERS TO CHAPTER 4 QUESTIONS

1. **What is the definition of play?**

   An activity that is for pure enjoyment and recreation without any formal, practical or serious purpose.

2. **What is a "Duchenne" smile and what makes it unique to any other type of facial expression?**

   A "Duchenne smile" is characterized by curling the muscles along the side of the mouth to such a degree as to show teeth as well as contraction of the muscles along the sides of the eyes. A "less-than-genuine" smile is void of much tooth exposure and eye contraction.

3. **In studies related to adolescents, laughter decreased three particular stress hormones and fortified the activity of the natural killer (NK) cells effectively keeping the immune system strong. What were these stress hormones?**

   Beta-endorphins, catecholamines and corticotropins

4. **List some examples of how children's hospitals, pediatric wards, and pedodontic offices are incorporating playfulness and humor to help reduce anxiety and promote wellness in children:**

   Various potential answers

5. **How does maintaining an appropriate level of fun and humor in the classroom benefit students?**

   Builds student-teacher connection, reduces anxiety, enhances learning process, greater academic satisfaction, provide psychological safety and better absorb the material

6. **What are some ways in which humor/laughter can help build longevity and manage relationship conflict?**

   - Humor promotes resiliency by taking difficult issues in stride and without anger
   - Gentle humor can be used to address sensitive issues
   - Playfulness and humor creates a bond between people
   - Laughter helps people loosen up, inspires more open-minded thinking
   - Playful settings disarm defensiveness
   - Inhibitions are released during periods of humor and laughter
   - Tension can be eased during a power struggle and help regain perspective

7. **Among older adults, what is the most common neurodegenerative disorder and what is the most common affective disorder?**

   Alzheimer's disease and depression, respectively

## ANSWERS TO CHAPTER 5 QUESTIONS

1. **True or false: Bowlby, a British psychologist, argues our need to bond with others is more fundamental to basic needs then our physiological requirements.**

   TRUE

2. **Why are attachment and bonding moments during and after birth important to relationship development?**

   The first experiences prime a baby's brain and body responses for a lifetime. These early bonding moments forge what researchers believe are early personality development and nonverbal communication between the infant and mother. This environment sets the stage for attachment, which is imperative for survival in and out of the womb. Human beings differ from most mammal species by coming into this world helpless and dependent on others for our continuance. If we are ignored, isolated, or disregarded by our caregivers we surely will die. In the womb you are already learning how to engage, build, and sustain relationships that will be required throughout your lifetime. Forming and developing healthy relationships with others is fundamental for human development.

3. **The Polyvagal Theory assumes all of the following EXCEPT:**

   a. **functions, organizes and interprets social behavior**

   b. **assists us to communicate with the environment**

   c. **automatically assumes everyone is a friend**

   d. **prepares the body for emergency mobilization**

   Answer: C

4. **Discuss one common characteristic in a healthy relationship that you find particularly important. Why is it so important to you?**

   Answers will vary.

5. **Healthy relationships are based on equality and respect not power and control. Why is this so important?**

   Human beings are on a quest for safety and we use others (in reciprocity) to feel safe and calm. The perception of safety is the turning point in the development of relationships. If we feel unsafe our brain sends a message to "flee—flight or fight" and we shut down because we identify risk factors that make it impossible for us to "trust" the other.

6. **Describe examples of behaviors found in unhealthy relationships.**

   You know you are in an unhealthy relationship when you walk away from someone and feel really bad about yourself (not once but again and again, time after time). You don't feel safe. You are always looking over your shoulder or have a feeling of needing to be "on guard." Another behavior found in unhealthy relationships is when you are called names that are unpleasant or others try and manipulate you or make you do something you don't want to do. Fear is another big warning sign—you are afraid to say what you think, to express your feelings without expecting retaliation or find yourself "walking on eggshells" because you fear how the other person will react to you. Pushing, grabbing, hitting, punching, or throwing objects are also common in unhealthy relationships. Another example is your partner controls you by having all the money or resources. You are dependent on them for everything. Blackmail, threats, ultimatums are also behaviors found in unhealthy relationships.

**7. Why is the ACE (Adverse Childhood Experiences) study so important? How does trauma impact healthy relationships?**

The ACE Study demonstrated there is a strong relationship between the ACE Score and a wide array of health and social problems throughout the lifespan. The ACE Study showed how childhood stressors affect the structure and function of the brain. The ACE Study suggests the more categories of trauma we experience in childhood the greater the likelihood of experiencing alcoholism, depression, illicit drug use, and partner violence; all of which directly impact our success at sustaining healthy relationships.

**8. We are "hard-wired" to be in relationships with one another because:**
   **a. we need connection to other people in order to thrive**
   **b. relationships affirm we have purpose and a role in the world**
   **c. relationships promote personal well-being**
   **d. we need to believe we make a difference in the world**
   **e. relationships give us a sense of "safety" and "survival"**
   **f. all of the above**
   Answer: F

# ANSWERS TO CHAPTER 6 QUESTIONS

1. What is the definition of nature?

   Various potential answers.

**2. What is the four-step guide to mindfully experiencing nature?**
   1. Acknowledging the moment in nature fully

   2. Intentionally paying attention to that moment and opening the senses

   3. Accepting all that nature is offering to the senses without judgment

   4. Making a cognitive choice to allow nature to have a positive impact

3. **Give an example of a structured outdoor activity and an unstructured outdoor activity.**

   Various potential answers.

4. **What are three traits that natural outdoor environments offer children when they play?**

   1. Unending diversity

   2. Not created by adults

   3. The feeling of timelessness.

5. **Define** *biophilia*.

   Humans have a subconscious connectivity with nature and activities/objects in a natural surrounding.

6. **What is the difference between the Limbic System and the Prefrontal Cortex?**

   The Limbic System is the first to develop and is the center for instinctual and emotional reaction. Commonly referred to as "the social brain," this area is responsible for emotional impulses, self-ishness, risk-taking behavior and primitive motivation. This area of the brain does not change with time and is formative.

   The Prefrontal Cortex is not fully matured until the early twenties and is the "reflective brain," where we find the hard-wired skills of thought differentiation, response inhibition, emotional regulation, prediction of outcomes, social control and organization. This part of the brain is the "grey matter" that actually develops over time and is able to be formed by learning and experience.

7. **According to the U.S. Census Bureau, what are the primary leisure activities that adults engage in?**

   Socializing, watching television, and engaging in computer-assisted activities.

## ANSWERS TO CHAPTER 7 QUESTIONS

1. **What is the difference between a predatory and a prey animal?**

   Various answers. Predators will seek their own food and attack to survive. Prey animals travel in groups or herds for survival and possess a strong "flight" response when frightened.

2. **What are some of the benefits of Animal Assisted Therapy to a patient/client?**

   Enhance physical, emotional, cognitive, and social function, improve fine motor skills, increase self-esteem, decrease anxiety, develop social skills, provide palliative care for patients undergoing chemotherapy, aid long-term care facility residents, assist veterans with Post-Traumatic Stress, assist mental health patients, improve fine motor skills

3. **What is the definition of an Animal Assisted Activity?**

Casual activities where an animal, its handler and an individual or group of individuals interact for comfort or recreational purposes

4. **In reference to the human-animal relationship, how does a horse differ from a house pet?**

Various answers

5. **Explain your understanding of the difference between the sympathetic and parasympathetic nervous systems?**

Fight or flight response versus relaxed, stress-free state of being

6. **Which do animals respond to: emotion or logic?**

Emotion

# Epilogue

*Photo courtesy of Maria Napoli*

You have completed your journey through *Whole Person Health: Mindfulness Across the Lifespan.* You may have realized that each day you begin a new journey holding many surprises, events, and emotions. Life is this way. We remember the road we have traveled on throughout our lives and embrace each step as we move forward, creating new memories, adventures, and relationships. Your happiness begins with the decisions you make and how you show up for the outcome of those decisions. Deepening your mindfulness practice, as you may have already experienced, will bring you more joy in all areas of your life. When we do not hold onto negative emotions and are able to let go of expectations, we open up hours, days, and weeks of more time for increasing quality in all areas of our life. You hopefully have dedicated more time to those areas of your life that have been neglected and maybe never explored. Find time to play, reflect, and listen and most of all do everything you do with love.

Take a moment to review the "My Whole Person Health" diagram that you filled out in the Prologue. Now take a moment and fill out "My Whole Person Health" diagram below. Once again, begin with 100% and designate how much of your time is spent in each life activity. Use the arrows to designate the percent. Do not forget to include how mindful you are. Notice the changes from the diagram you filled out at the beginning. What decisions have you made? What is the next step toward living the life of your dreams? Make a commitment to yourself to live in the moment, embracing each experience. It is your life, your destiny, your journey!

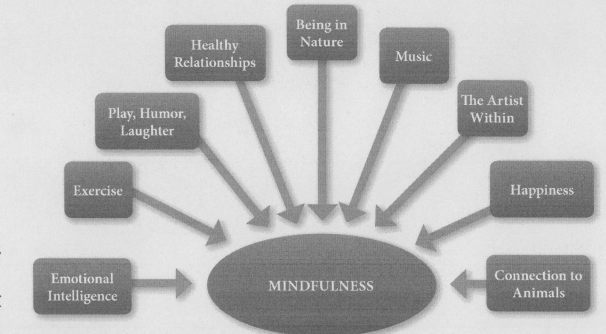

*Courtesy of Maria Napoli*